My Cute Daughter

My Cu†e Daughter

A Devotional Diary

PAT NOBLE

Point Press
PO Box 299181
Pembroke Pines, FL 33029
daryljones.org/pointpress

Cover Design by Allyson Rhodes

Edited by Gabe Smith

Printed in the United States of America.

ISBN # 978-1-7372230-4-7

Endorsements

"Imagine giving your daughter or any special lady in your life words of encouragement that strengthen her sense of value and worth in the Lord—words that help her live a joyous and successful life based on Biblical truth. Now imagine writing these words down so that they can become a cherished treasure for her that she can revisit from time to time throughout her life. That gift of love is this devotional diary, written by my friend, Pat Noble. It is unique, timely, relevant, and lasting. Rich with Scripture and sound principles, this diary provides a legacy of love."

DR. TONY EVANS

Senior Pastor, Oak Cliff Bible Fellowship | President, The Urban Alternative

"With so many conflicting messages about identity, image, and purpose in our society, it is imperative that we look to God for answers. My Cute Daughter is an amazing resource for women of all ages. These devotionals are a wonderful tool for women to grow in knowing the Lord's will and purpose for their lives. The Bible is also clear that parents are ultimately responsible for the discipleship of their children. My Cute Daughter is a wonderful resource for fathers, as well as mothers to use with their daughters so that they grow in knowing who the Lord is and His plans for their lives."

DR. DARYL JONES

Senior Pastor, The Rock Fellowship Church | President, Point Ministries

"In a culture that banks on outward beauty and seemingly endless achievement, Pat Noble gently leads her readers toward peace. Her tried-and-true year of devotions leads us to consider inward strength & authentic beauty anchored in steadfast love that resides deep in our souls, a gift from our Creator, our adoring audience of One. Dare we receive such love? Dare we believe such beauty? Pat's encouragement, alongside inspiring stories and thoughtful prompts, invites mothers and daughters to grow in Truth, together. A special time that will always be a treasure (even in life's trials)."

KAY WILLS WYMA

Author of The Peace Project

"Having lost my mother before knowing my worth as a woman and my identity in Christ, a diary like this would have been a treasured gift through the decades of silence without her. It would have been a tattered reference guide, alongside my bible, because I would have read it again and again.

There are times in everyone's life when we need to be reminded of our value through the eyes of a trusted loved one. I can imagine readers returning to the words written in this diary through the seasons of their lives. It lovingly reminds us of our worth as daughters of the Most High King. What a treasure Pat Noble has prepared for others to give to a daughter, niece, or loved one, that will transcend time. My Cute Daughter, a Devotional Diary is a gift for the giver as much as it is for the Cute Daughters who will receive it."

BRENDA TEELE
Television Personality

Dedication

To my granddaughters
Noah Renee and Mathai Selah
My prayer is that this devotional diary will help you realize how
"fearfully and wonderfully made" you are
so that you will live life fully as the masterpieces God created you to be.
I hope this diary becomes **a cherished treasure** of love
from God, me, Poppy, your dad, and your mom.
Nana Cute loves you so so much!

Acknowledgments

I am forever grateful for my family and many friends who helped me during the process of working on this devotional diary. Your prayers and words of encouragement, despite many obstacles, kept me moving forward.

I owe a special debt of gratitude to my son, Ryan Noble. After hearing what the Holy Spirit laid on my heart based on what my father did for me, he encouraged me to pursue this project. Ryan's countless hours spent with me deliberating over the content and Scriptures, his biblical insights, and his wisdom were priceless. We have worked on so many projects together, and despite the challenges and dynamics of a mom and son relationship, we enjoy working together. Thank you, Ryan. I love you so, so much.

I want to especially thank my editor, Gabe Smith, for your enthusiasm to take on this project. Thank you for all of your feedback, corrections, suggestions, insights, and careful work during the editing process. Your eyes caught my mistakes, and your suggestions made the diary better. You have a wonderful gift, and the Lord directed me to the right person.

Thank you, Sylvia Stewart, Brenda Teele, and Anne Haynes, for your constant encouragement of my gifts. Your eagle eyes and insightful feedback on the impact of the diary and your assistance with the design of the cover helped to deliver the finished product. I can always depend upon your honesty with my work.

Thank you, Allyson Rhodes, for designing the cover of the diary. I know I threw a few curve balls your way, yet you caught them and your creativity delivered the vision.

Thank you, Point Press, for accepting this assignment and helping me to publish this work. Kamica Jones, your patience, dedication, and knowledge of the publishing process made this journey a very smooth one. You are truly a gifted lady and dear friend.

To my husband, Tony, and family—Branden, Dani, Noah, Mathai, and Judge. Thank you for your patience with me. I know my projects add a little chaos to your lives, yet you allow me to fulfill my calling and love me through the process. I love you all so, so much.

Thank you to everyone who constantly encouraged me to use my God-given gifts, especially when I failed to see them or want to give up. There are too many to name, but you know who you are.

Finally, to my dad, Pastor Charles L. Jackson, who is with the Lord. Thank you, daddy, for the cherished treasure you left me which inspired this diary. Your impact is still reaching others for Christ.

How to Use this Book

This diary contains fifty-two weekly devotionals to be shared with a young lady or woman age fourteen and beyond. It can be a parent with a daughter, a mentor with a mentee, or basically any mature person with a younger lady.

This diary can be used alone, but the intended purpose is to walk through it with a more mature Christian. The devotionals are designed to be shared between you and the recipient of this diary. Begin by writing the recipient's name, your name, and the date in the lines provided on the next few pages. Although it may be different from the diary you are accustomed to using, this devotional diary will become **a cherished treasure**.

Each week's devotional imparts words of wisdom to help you live successfully. Proverbs 2:4-6 says:

> *"If you seek her as silver,*
> *And search for her as for hidden treasures;*
> *Then you will discern the fear of the Lord,*
> *And discover the knowledge of God.*
> *For the Lord gives wisdom;*
> *From His mouth come knowledge and understanding."*

The devotionals, designed to be completed in as little as fifteen to twenty minutes, can extend far beyond that timeframe based on the richness of the conversation. The topic material can be tweaked and adjusted depending on the age of the recipient.

Three questions accompany each devotional to spark a conversation around the topic for the week. However, conversations can go much deeper and can extend to other topics, so feel free to use your own questions as well.

After discussing the questions, a section titled **My Cute Daughter** completes the devotional. This is the place where **you** can write words of encouragement related to the devotional topic to the recipient of this diary. The recipient may read what you wrote and keep the book until the next week or you may prefer to keep it depending on the age of the recipient.

After completion of the year and all fifty-two devotionals, the diary is presented to the recipient as a keepsake. It becomes **a cherished treasure** when life hits or she faces challenges. The devotionals, packed rich with Scripture, allow her to refer back to what her Heavenly Father and you wrote to encourage her. It becomes a diary of love to her from God and you.

A Cherished Treasure

The inspiration of this devotional diary came from an act of love by my earthly father, Pastor Charles Lee Jackson. After experiencing the death of my baby daughter and first child, Shawn, I struggled to make sense of it all. I questioned God on why He took her away, and I felt lost. I started sinking into depression and wrote my daddy a letter asking him questions I failed to understand. My dad responded with a three-page epistle with answers from our Heavenly Father, which started the healing process I desperately needed.

Today, I still cherish that letter written forty years ago. Even though it is old, torn, and weathered on the edges, I read it on occasion to remind me of his love for me during a difficult time in my life. My father has since gone home to be with the Lord, but the words of encouragement from our Heavenly Father and him remain **a cherished treasure**. A copy of the letter he wrote follows below.

This Devotional Diary belongs
to

_____

Given in love
from

_____

On

_____

The Theme

The theme throughout this diary reveals how much Jesus truly loves you. You are His "fearfully and wonderfully made" daughter. He gave you gifts and talents to use for His purpose and His glory. If you use them wisely, you will live a successful life.

And if you truly trust Him and remain under His protective care, He promised in Hebrews 13:5 to "*never leave you or forsake you.*"

Why? Simply because you are

Cu✝e...
Covered Until The End

Table of Contents

There Can Never Be a More Beautiful You
Artificial Cuteness

*"I will give **thanks** to You, for I am fearfully and wonderfully made"*
Psalm 139:14a (emphasis added)

The world demands that you must possess certain physical attributes to be considered beautiful, accepted, loved, or successful. To make matters worse, when young ladies fail to fit this definition of "cute," many of them search for "artificial cuteness."

Contrary to popular belief, the typical American woman does not wear a size 2. In fact, the average American dress size falls between 11 and 14. Yet, in our culture, if you wear a size 0-6, have a certain hair texture and skin tone, you are somehow destined to be beautiful, successful, and happy. But these standards represent lies our culture wants you to believe.

Young ladies will go to extremes trying to accomplish these unrealistic standards of beauty. They spend countless hours and dollars searching for all kinds of weight loss products, lotions, gels, sprays, and make-up trying to mold and make themselves into versions of "artificial cuteness."

Sometimes we look at female idols to determine beauty. We think they arrived in this world flawless, not realizing that cosmetologists, makeup artists, estheticians, and graphic designers use tools of the trade like airbrushes, lighting, and photoshop to help make these women look perfect. In the real world, women do not walk with an army of "beautifiers" everywhere they go. However, these artificial beauties tend to shape the self-worth of many women.

Contrary to what the world promotes as beauty, God created you absolutely beautiful, accepted, successful, loved, cared for, worthy, and so much more. No matter your physical attributes, you represent His amazing creation. You are His **Cu7e** daughter, "fearfully and wonderfully made" (Psalm 139:14). So, give thanks to the Lord because He formed you and shaped you just the way He wanted you. He loves what He created and never makes mistakes. He tailor-made only one of you and in His eyes, there can never be a more beautiful you!

Christian singer Jonny Diaz's song, *A More Beautiful You*, reminds us whose perception really matters.

> Little girl fourteen flipping through a magazine,
> Says she wants to look that way
> But her hair isn't straight her body isn't fake
> And she's always felt overweight
>
> Well little girl fourteen I wish that you could see
> That beauty is within your heart
> And you were made with such care your skin your body and your hair
> Are perfect just the way they are
>
> There could never be a more beautiful you
> Don't buy the lies, disguises and hoops, they make you jump through
> You were made to fill a purpose that only you could do
> So there could never be a more beautiful you[i]

Discussion Points

1. What does the term "artificial cuteness" mean to you?

   _____

   _____

   _____

2. What standards of beauty exist in our culture today? What erroneous things do young ladies do in order to be "beautiful?"

   _____

   _____

   _____

3. Why should we give thanks to the Lord for our outward appearance?

   _____

   _____

   _____

My Cu*f*e Daughter

_____
_____
_____
_____
_____
_____
_____
_____
_____
_____
_____
_____

Covered Until The End

A Beautiful Piece of Art
Fearfully and Wonderfully Made

*"I will give thanks to You, for I am **fearfully** and **wonderfully** made…"*
Psalm 139:14a (emphasis added)

The word fearful usually indicates a sense of dread, panic, terror, or an anticipation of danger. However, it can also express profound awe or reverence.

Do you fear your mother or father? If you grew up like me as a child, I feared my parents, but I never lived in terror of them. Even though they did administer Godly discipline, my parents were not monsters, and I never anticipated danger for my life. They lived out their faith and instructed me in the Word of God.

I feared my parents because I carried such reverence and awe for them and wished to avoid disappointing them. I tried hard not to break their hearts over something I said or did. I highly honored and respected them.

Because you are fearfully made, you ought to live your life in such a manner that people will revere you. The reflection of your Heavenly Father portrayed throughout your life represents an admiring fear. He regards you as worthy of great honor and respect.

What do you think of when you hear the word wonderful? A delicious food? An inspiring vista? An amazing vacation getaway? God designed you in a wonderful way to fulfill His purpose and give Him glory. When He looks at you, He is in awe of His creation. You are His marvelous daughter.

God did not haphazardly throw you together. Genesis 2:7 says, "Then the Lord God formed man of dust from the ground." Yet, when He created woman, Genesis 2:22 says, "The Lord God fashioned into a woman the rib which He had taken from the man." The word "fashioned" is from the Hebrew word *banah* and means "to build." The word was used for making forms of art, a temple, or even constructing palaces. It implies that a woman's design showcases an aesthetic work of art. In other words, God deliberately constructed a woman as a visually pleasing, invaluable, work of art.

Wow! He "fashioned" you with His imagination and ingenuity. He made you a beautiful piece of art. Look at the unique bodies He created—the variations of hues, shapes, and sizes. Look at all the personalities, skills, and talents women possess.

A comical saying goes like this, "God made man and said, 'It is good, but I can do better.' And then He made woman!" So, every day and everywhere you go, you display His imagination and ingenuity. You are His **Cu†e** daughter, fearfully and wonderfully made.

Discussion Points

1. Do you fear your mom or dad? Why? Give an example of something you did and how you felt scared when your parent(s) found out. What happened?

   _____

   _____

   _____

2. What comes to mind when you hear the word wonderful? What aspects or features make it wonderful?

   _____

   _____

   _____

3. What does it mean to be "fearfully and wonderfully" made?

   _____

   _____

   _____

My Cu†e Daughter

_____

_____

_____

_____

_____

_____

_____

_____

_____

_____

Covered Until The End

Spirit, Soul, Body
The Connection

"I will give thanks to You, for I am fearfully and wonderfully made;
Wonderful are Your works, and my soul knows it very well."
Psalm 139:14

"Now may the God of peace Himself sanctify you entirely; and may your spirit and soul and body be
preserved complete, without blame at the coming of our Lord Jesus Christ."
1 Thessalonians 5:23

We often hear the well-known expression "body and soul," but God gave us three components: spirit, soul, and body. Notice God places spirit first, soul next, and body last in 1 Thessalonians 5:23. The order signifies importance.

The spirit represents the most important component of you. In Greek and Hebrew, the translation of the word spirit refers to "wind, blow, and breath." The connection between spirit and the Holy Spirit becomes clearer in Genesis 2:7, "Then the Lord God formed man of dust from the ground and breathed into his nostrils the breath of life; and man became a living being."

The second component, your soul, consists of your intellect, will, and sensibility. The Greek word for soul, *psyche*, refers to the "inner, immaterial essence of human beings." Your soul consists of your personality, your feelings, your emotions—the complex characteristics that distinguish one individual from another. In other words, your soul makes you, "you"!

Your body makes up the third and final component of your being. The Greek translation *soma* refers to the material part of you—your physical parts and appearance.

Let's connect the three components in the last part of Psalm 139:14 that says "and my soul knows it very well." What does your soul know very well? That you are "fearfully and wonderfully made."

The spirit, soul, body connection works like this. God's Word says it and then the Holy Spirit puts it in your spirit. Your soul responds to your spirit. You believe it, you accept it as truth, and your thoughts and emotions align with His Word.

You feel fearfully and wonderfully made. You think fearful and wonderful thoughts about yourself. Your body starts to respond to your soul. You start walking and talking like a masterpiece. You dance and sing like a masterpiece. In fact, your ears will not accept anything contrary to this truth. Now you experience the spirit, soul, and body connection.

God doesn't want you to just know it, He wants you to know it very well! He wants His Word firmly planted in your spirit so it penetrates your soul and affects your body. In other words, He wants you to feed your heart with His truths because what flows from your heart will affect your soul and body.

Discussion Points

1. Give an example of the spirit, soul, body connection.

   _____

   _____

   _____

2. Name some things that you should reject because they represent lies contrary to what God says about you.

   _____

   _____

   _____

3. What makes you, "you?" Can you say that your soul "knows it very well?" Why?

   _____

   _____

   _____

My Cu †e Daughter

_____

_____

_____

_____

_____

_____

_____

_____

_____

_____

_____

Covered Until The End

Cultivate a Beautiful Heart
Inward Beauty

"But the fruit of the Spirit is love, joy, peace, patience, kindness, goodness, faithfulness, gentleness, self-control; against such things there is no law."
Galatians 5:22-23

"Watch over your heart with all diligence,
For from it flow the springs of life."
Proverbs 4:23

A quote by Helen Keller says, "The best and most beautiful things in the world cannot be seen or even touched. They must be felt with the heart." These words of wisdom came from a lady with no earthly sight but gifted in divine insight. She knew the real meaning of beauty—it's a heart thing.

Throughout generations, mothers echoed the familiar phrase "beauty is only skin deep." But genuine beauty depicts much more than what lies on the outside. True beauty evolves not from lotions, gels, or jars. You can't paint it on your lips or brush it on your eyes and cheeks. You can't surgically implant, tuck, or pluck it. True beauty comes from the inside out.

As Scripture reveals, outward beauty fades. So don't spend all your time perfecting the outward body. God looks at your inner being—your heart. The challenge then becomes how beautiful is your heart, your inner spirit? The Holy Spirit feeds the heart of a beautiful woman. Her heart pumps the fruit of the Spirit found in Galatians 5:22-23: love, joy, peace, patience, kindness, goodness, faithfulness, gentleness, and self-control.

Continue to read and meditate on the Word of God. Feed your heart with God's truth. That way, when faced with adverse situations, the Holy Spirit will breathe the appropriate Word of God back to you.

It's a heart thing. No matter how you try to dress things up, change or re-arrange your outward looks, Jesus seeks a beautiful heart. So what do you allow into your heart? What the world, the media, or other people say about you? Do you allow what you say about you? Or do you allow what God says about you to penetrate your heart?

What's hidden in your heart will show up in your thoughts and feelings. But if you don't hide God's Word in your heart, then you will never feel the beauty that He sees nor will your heart look beautiful to Him. He's looking for women with beautiful hearts.

Proverbs 4:23 says, "Watch over your heart with all diligence, for from it flow the springs of life." Truth, not fact, brings life. Here's an example. Fact: You may feel lonely. Truth: Hebrews 13:5 reminds you that God will never leave nor forsake you. So, feed your heart with God's truth. Remember, what flows from your heart will affect your soul and body.

The woman who knows the meaning of true beauty gives the same or more meticulous attention to cultivating her inward beauty that she gives to her outward beauty. Proverbs 31:30 reminds us "Charm is deceitful, and beauty is vain, but a woman who fears the Lord, she shall be praised." Your true beauty comes from your inner being. Cultivate a beautiful heart.

Discussion Points

1. Why should you spend more time on your inward beauty than your outward beauty?

   _____

   _____

   _____

2. Which areas involving the fruit of the Spirit (love, joy, peace, patience, kindness, etc.) represent strengths for you? Which areas do you need to improve?

   _____

   _____

   _____

3. Why must you watch over your heart with diligence?

   _____

   _____

   _____

My Cu†e Daughter

_____
_____
_____
_____
_____
_____
_____
_____
_____
_____
_____

Covered Until The End

Love Your Beautiful Body
Outward Beauty

"Charm is deceitful and beauty is vain;
But a woman who fears the Lord, she shall be praised."
Proverbs 31:30

Beauty—the color and fragrance of a blooming red rose, the crystal-clear sparkling blue water on a tropical island, the brilliant hues of the rainbow after a summer thunderstorm. These beautiful images portray qualities that give pleasure to the senses. However, in our culture, the term beauty often describes physical attractiveness.

Most ladies feel uncomfortable calling themselves beautiful simply because they buy into the culture's definition of beauty. They focus on the models in the magazines and fail to measure up to their standards. They also forget that a model's career tends to be short-lived. Most models only stick around for 2-5 years, then the industry moves on to the next ones. But God never tosses you out. He created your outward appearance and loves every inch of you.

The impact of these images on the self-worth of young women is devastating. Young girls develop negative thoughts about themselves when they fail to measure up to the image of idols. Without proper guidance and truth, they start to make unrealistic comparisons. Mix in peer pressure, along with media influence, and the devastation increases. You ultimately end up with young ladies who become confused, desiring disproportionate body figures.

Love the beautiful body God gave you. Stop comparing yourself to how someone else thinks you should look. They did not create you. If you desire to make improvements to look and feel your best, go ahead and do it. There's nothing wrong with touch-ups or enhancements. Just stop wasting time trying to live up to other people's standards of beauty. And don't try to change the original design of the artist. God created you in the image of His Son, and no matter how you try to dress things up, change things around, or rearrange things, you will still remain you. And God says, "My **Cute** daughter, you are a sight to behold."

Discussion Points

1. On a scale of 1 to 10 (1 signifying "not attractive at all" and 10 signifying "out-of-the-box gorgeous"), how would you rate yourself? Why?

   _____

   _____

   _____

2. What does the statement mean: "Don't try to change the original design of the artist"? Give examples of design changes pertaining to your body. Give an example of making an improvement to a part of His original design of your body.

   _____

   _____

   _____

3. How does media, social, and peer pressure contribute to the comparison trap?

   _____

   _____

   _____

My Cu†e Daughter

_____

_____

_____

_____

_____

_____

_____

_____

_____

_____

_____

Honoring Your Body
Healthy Body

"Or do you not know that your body is a temple of the Holy Spirit who is in you, whom you have from God, and that you are not your own? For you have been bought with a price; therefore, glorify God in your body."
1 Corinthians 6:19-20

A lot of our attention focuses on keeping the body fit and trim. Thousands of health food diets, fads, body building gyms, and cosmetic surgeries compete for your dollars to improve your body. Now, there is absolutely nothing wrong with improving your body and looking good. Just do it for the right reasons. Will God love you more if you lose or gain ten pounds? No, He loves you just the way you are, right now! Don't allow the fitness craze to consume you.

God gave you a wonderful gift—your body. He wants you to respect and honor it by taking care of the body He designed. Cherish, preserve, and improve your health if needed, because the way you treat your body will determine to some degree the richness and quality of your life.

The apostle Paul reminds you in 1 Corinthians 6:19 that your body is a temple of the Holy Spirit, so give the Spirit your best by not neglecting it. See, God wants to use your body as an instrument for ministry. Your hands, arms, legs, feet, eyes, ears, smiles—indeed, every part of your physical existence—can minister for His glory.

God had a divine design in mind when He created you! Give your body the best treatment so you can live out a full, meaningful, and productive life. Make your temple, your body, a great place for the Holy Spirit to live!

Discussion Points

1. What do you like about your body?

    _____

    _____

    _____

2. Name some characteristics of your body that you would change. Why? How will you change them?

    _____

    _____

    _____

3. What does the following statement mean: "The way you treat your body will determine to some degree the richness and quality of your life"?

    _____

    _____

    _____

My Cu†e Daughter

_____

_____

_____

_____

_____

_____

_____

_____

_____

_____

_____

Covered Until The End

God's Masterpiece
One of a Kind

*"For we are His **workmanship**, created in Christ Jesus for good works, which God prepared beforehand so that we would walk in them."*
Ephesians 2:10 (emphasis added)

"I will never desert you nor will I ever forsake you."
Hebrews 13:5

God made you a one-of-a-kind masterpiece! Even Leonardo da Vinci could not come close to creating or reproducing you. God called you His workmanship, His piece of art. He marvels at your distinct qualities, and as He beholds you, He gets great satisfaction. He adores His work of art because you bear the image of His Son.

The Mona Lisa resides in a museum as a piece of art widely considered a masterpiece. The exquisite artwork evokes emotions as you consider the hand of the artist and his skill in creating it. This unique, one-of-a-kind picture is meticulously cared for, protected, and preserved by the curators in the museum.

You exist in this world as a piece of art created with extraordinary skill by the supreme artist— your Heavenly Father. You represent God's masterpiece and the value He places on you goes beyond any monetary amount. He promised to take care of you, protect you, provide for all your needs, and preserve you for His glory and enjoyment. You are His **Cu†e** daughter, and He promised to Cover You Until The End.

The great wonder lies in the fact that He made no duplication of you. He created an unrepeatable masterpiece! In this entire world, only one of you exists!

Discussion Points

1. Describe the emotion you feel when you gaze on an amazing painting or piece of art.

   _____

   _____

   _____

2. What distinct qualities do you possess that make you unique?

   _____

   _____

   _____

3. How do you feel knowing you are a one-of-a-kind masterpiece?

   _____

   _____

   _____

My Cu*te Daughter

_____

_____

_____

_____

_____

_____

_____

_____

_____

_____

_____

_____

A Piece of the Puzzle
Uniquely Designed for a Purpose

"Now you are Christ's body, and individually members of it."
1 Corinthians 12:27

Ever worked on a puzzle? How do you put the pieces of the puzzle together? Most people normally start off with all the parts scattered across the floor or table. You try to look at the shapes and colors of each piece to see where they fit into the overall puzzle.

If you try to place the wrong piece into the wrong part of the puzzle, it doesn't work. You can try to force it, but it will mess up another piece or the entire puzzle. You will get frustrated and possibly not complete it.

The reason the piece needs to fit in the correct place stems from the fact that it has been uniquely designed to fit in that exact spot. It represents the right size, shape, and color, so it fits perfectly into the puzzle to create the picture on the box. When all the pieces fit into their specific spaces, the puzzle emerges complete. Now you reveal a beautiful picture that resembles the image on the box.

This holds true for each of us. You have been uniquely designed with the right size, shape, and color to fulfill your divine purpose. If you try to change or alter your design, you live a frustrated and unfulfilled life. Paul writes in 1 Corinthians 12:27, "Now you are Christ's body, and individually members of it."

Your unique design resembles a piece of God's puzzle. When you fulfill your divine purpose, you fit perfectly into the puzzle of God's family. When all the pieces fit together, a beautiful picture of the image of heaven emerges.

Discussion Points

1. What does it mean to be uniquely designed?

   _____

   _____

   _____

2. How do you feel when you can't get a puzzle piece to fit in a spot you try to put it in? What do you do? What do you think will happen if you try to change or alter your unique design?

   _____

   _____

   _____

3. Based on your uniqueness, how might you use it to fulfill your divine purpose?

   _____

   _____

   _____

My Cu†e Daughter

_____

_____

_____

_____

_____

_____

_____

_____

_____

_____

Covered Until The End

Seek God First

Priorities

"But seek first His kingdom and His righteousness, and all these things will be added to you."
Matthew 6:33

Hundreds of possibilities exist in this life. Each day you choose from among the numerous options vying for your attention. Choosing one thing over something else proves sometimes difficult. You only get 24 hours in a day and more things to do than time allows. So, to maintain sanity, you must decide what takes precedence. In other words, you must prioritize.

What do you do? God's Word reveals the answer: "But seek first His kingdom and His righteousness, and all these things will be added to you." In effect, here lies your priority. When you put God first—spending time with Him and getting to know Him—everything else tends to fall into place. More work gets accomplished, the right work gets done, and a sense of peace resides within you.

See, if you run around too busy to seek Him, then you are busier than He wants you to be. God never gives you busy work to take away time from knowing Him. So, this means all your decisions should come to Him. The decisions related to your job, education, mate or future mate, money, home or whatever, need to reflect His kingdom and righteousness. Everything and everybody else should occupy second place.

Chuck Swindoll coined a phrase: "Life is a lot like a coin; you can spend it any way you wish, but you can spend it only once." If you make Christ a priority in your life and seek Him first in all your decisions, your life will result in one well spent.

Discussion Points

1. What things can keep you from prioritizing God in your life? What do you need to do to get your priorities right?

   _____

   _____

   _____

2. What decisions do you need to seek His guidance on?

   _____

   _____

   _____

3. What does the phrase mean: "Life is a lot like a coin; you can spend it any way you wish, but you can spend it only once"?

   _____

   _____

   _____

My Cu†e Daughter

_____

_____

_____

_____

_____

_____

_____

_____

_____

_____

_____

Covered Until The End

Modesty in Dress
Dress

"Likewise, I want women to adorn themselves with proper clothing, modestly and discreetly, not with braided hair and gold or pearls or costly garments…"
1 Timothy 2:9

We live in a culture plagued by immodesty. Whether in dress, speech, or behavior, the guiding principle of life seems to scream, "It's your thing; do what you want to do." But God commands a different viewpoint on this topic. In regards to dress, His Word stands clear: "Likewise, I want women to adorn themselves with proper clothing, modestly and discreetly…"

I attended a wedding of a friend where one of the guests dressed like a stripper. Not only did her clothes fit too tight for her large body frame, but they neglected to appropriately cover certain body parts. People gawked as she flaunted among the wedding party. Her negative portrayal of herself took away the focus from the bride and interrupted the flow of the reception. She became a distraction.

Many women with small and large body frames possess beautiful outward features. Sadly, it proves often hard to see their beauty due to the tight-fitting, cleavage-baring, and booty-revealing clothes that cheapens them. They get so caught up in the world's standards of beauty that they end up looking like women of the "night" rather than God's women of the "light."

Will they get stares? Will they be the center of conversation? Will they fit in with the world's standards? Absolutely! Will they represent part of the "in-crowd"? No doubt about it. However, the real questions emerge: What will the Lord say when He sees His daughters dressed in this manner? How will God measure them against His image of a godly woman?

Discussion Points

1. What does it mean to dress modestly and discreetly?

   _____

   _____

   _____

2. How do you think the Lord feels about His daughters dressing immodestly?

   _____

   _____

   _____

3. What image comes to mind when you think of a Godly woman?

   _____

   _____

   _____

My Cu†e Daughter

_____

_____

_____

_____

_____

_____

_____

_____

_____

_____

_____

Covered Until The End

Modesty in Speech Part 1
Speech

"Let no unwholesome word proceed from your mouth, but only such a word as is good for edification according to the need of the moment, so that it may give grace to those who hear."
Ephesians 4:29

Sometimes situations and people test your limits especially in the area of speech. Be careful to choose your words wisely because they represent the doors to your heart. What empties out of your mouth flows from your heart. Your words convey your character so make sure they portray the correct picture of you.

In regards to speech, God's Word speaks clearly when faced with knowing what to say. Ephesians 5:4 says, "and there must be no filthiness and silly talk, or coarse jesting [harsh or crude joking], which are not fitting…" Proverbs 4:24 states, "Put away from you a deceitful mouth, and put devious lips far from you."

In college, my husband and I agreed to go on a double date with a friend of his and his girlfriend. When we met the young lady, her outward appearance gave a very favorable impression. But as soon as she opened her mouth, the beauty quickly vanished. The classic saying, "She curses like a sailor" fit her manner of speech.

The use of harsh words, cussing, crude jokes, and foul vulgar language says volumes about you. They diminish your beauty and value. Use words that edify others and glorify God.

Discussion Points

1. Give examples of some unwholesome words. Counter them with words that edify.

   _____

   _____

   _____

2. Why must you watch what you say?

   _____

   _____

   _____

3. How do you think God feels when we say mean and ugly things to someone?

   _____

   _____

   _____

My Cu*t*e Daughter

_____
_____
_____
_____
_____
_____
_____
_____
_____
_____
_____
_____

Modesty in Speech Part 2
Speech

"Let your speech always be with grace, as though seasoned with salt, so that you will know how you should respond to each person."
Colossians 4:6

Knowing what to say represents one aspect of our speech. Knowing how to say it poses an even greater challenge. In the 1960's, Dr. Albert Mehrabian led one of the most well-known research projects on nonverbal communication. He concluded that nonverbals represent 93% of our communication.

Nonverbal communication reveals what people say other than their spoken words. 55% of nonverbal communication involves body language (visuals) while 38% of a message gets communicated through tone and voice inflection (vocals). Words comprise only 7% of the message.

Body language involves such things as hand gestures, eye, head and facial movements, and posture. Tone and voice inflection involve emotions behind the words and emphasis placed on certain words. You can say the exact same words, but change the meaning behind them by simply emphasizing certain words. Pay attention to nonverbal communication when speaking. When nonverbals and words contradict, people read nonverbals.

Remember, you can speak the truth, but the manner in which you say it may hinder the reception of the message. Ephesians 4:15 reminds us to speak the truth in love. Carefully choose your words because once you say them, you will either build up or tear down. Also, make sure your nonverbal cues support your intended message and bring edification, not destruction.

Discussion Points

1. Say the word "oh" in a manner that expresses the following emotions. How did the word change?

    *Pleasure *Anger *Surprise *Disappointment *Understanding *Sarcasm

    _____

    _____

    _____

2. While saying the word "oh," what body language did you notice?

    _____

    _____

    _____

3. What does the Scripture mean when it says, "Let your speech always be with grace, as though seasoned with salt"? Give an example of bringing destruction to a message.

    _____

    _____

    _____

My Cu†e Daughter

_____

_____

_____

_____

_____

_____

_____

_____

_____

_____

_____

Covered **Until The End**

27

Modesty in Behavior
Behavior

"but like the Holy One who called you, be holy yourselves also in all your behavior..."
1 Peter 1:15

Your behavior or the manner in which you conduct yourself says volumes about you. How you carry yourself will determine to a large degree how others respect and respond to you. Living a holy lifestyle requires you to set yourself apart from the world's ways.

In regards to behavior, whether at home, school, work or play, your conduct should reflect God's standards. This relates to speaking, dressing, and acting in a proper manner that's pleasing to the Lord. God's Word speaks clearly when faced with knowing how to act. 1 Timothy 3:11 says, "Women must likewise be dignified, not malicious gossips, but temperate, faithful in all things." 1 Peter 2:12 urges you to "Keep your behavior excellent among the Gentiles..."

Living in this world requires that you interact with people driven by the world's system. You live in the world, but you don't have to be of the world. The world will tell you *just do it. Everyone else is doing it. You only live once. It's okay as long as it doesn't hurt anyone.*

These statements and others cause many to act improperly. You must make a decision to follow Him. It takes courage to stand alone from the crowd. But consistently pursuing godly behavior brings great pleasure to the Lord.

Discussion Points

1. What does the statement mean, "How you carry yourself will determine to a large degree how others respect and respond to you"?

   _____

   _____

   _____

2. What's an example of a worldly behavior—a behavior not of God?

   _____

   _____

   _____

3. Explain what it means to live in the world but not of the world.

   _____

   _____

   _____

My Cu*t*e Daughter

_____

_____

_____

_____

_____

_____

_____

_____

_____

_____

_____

Covered Until The End

Lifestyle of Excellence
Excellence

"Now, my daughter, do not fear. I will do for you whatever you ask, for all my people in the city know that you are a woman of excellence."
Ruth 3:11

"Now for this very reason also, applying all diligence, in your faith supply moral excellence, and in your moral excellence, knowledge…"
2 Peter 1:5

Maintaining the status quo and mediocrity reign in our times. Incompetence creeps in as an acceptable standard. No need to live differently in a society that accepts just getting by. It's easier to perform the same and swim like the rest.

The book of Ruth tells the story of a virtuous woman of excellence. She lived above the norm of her time. She showed loyal love to her mother-in-law, Naomi and the God Naomi served. When Ruth's husband died, she chose to stay with Naomi which involved leaving her culture, people, and language.

Even though this era in Ruth's time involved rebellion and immortality, Ruth lived a life of integrity and righteousness. She became known for excellence in her work, gleaning in the field, and her entire lifestyle. Her reputation of excellence led the owner Boaz to grant her favor. "Now, my daughter, do not fear. I will do for you whatever you ask, for all my people in the city know that you are a woman of excellence."

God calls us to live above mediocrity. He wants us to set a higher standard to impact and reshape our environment instead of waiting on someone else to set the pace. He wants us to live a lifestyle of excellence. Excellence creates greatness. It separates those who just want to get by from those who want to soar.

When you choose to live differently, you will face challenges. Striving for excellence may cause many people to view you as a threat since you will not blend in with the majority. When you refuse to "go with the flow," your popularity suffers. But the pursuit of excellence is crucial if you desire to live God's way and receive His favor.

Whatever you do, do it well. Make up your mind from the beginning of any endeavor that it will receive your very best. Never settle for average because it only places you equal distance from the bottom to the top. God desires a commitment to excellence in every part of our lives; work, relationships, ethical behavior, moral decisions, physical and spiritual upkeep.

Give God your best because He gave His best to you in the form of His Son, Jesus. Remember God is the One you must honor and please. He stands as the final appraiser of your lifestyle. Live like Ruth—a woman of excellence. God deserves your very best and nothing less.

Discussion Points

1. What specific things may happen to you when you do not "go with the flow"?

   _____

   _____

   _____

2. Why shouldn't you settle for just "getting by"? Name some things you can do to go beyond mediocrity.

   _____

   _____

   _____

3. What can you do as a woman to maintain a lifestyle of excellence?

   _____

   _____

   _____

My Cu†e Daughter

_____

_____

_____

_____

_____

_____

_____

_____

_____

_____

_____

Covered Until The End

Birds of a Feather

Influences

"Do not be deceived: 'Bad company corrupts good morals.'"
1 Corinthians 15:33

"A little leaven leavens the whole lump of dough."
Galatians 5:9

When my youngest granddaughter, Mathai, turned 9 months old, she started picking herself up and walking a few steps while holding on to something for support. Until she mastered walking on her own, she spent most of the time crawling or rolling around on the floor.

I noticed something very interesting from her older sister, Noah. My 2-year-old granddaughter started doing everything that Mathai did. If Mathai crawled, Noah got down and crawled with her. If Mathai rolled on her back, Noah followed suit. If Mathai cried, Noah burst into a dramatic scream.

It made me think of a familiar expression: "Birds of a feather flock together." At first glance, you may think this quote only applies to the bird species since you see geese flying in groups when the seasons change as they migrate together. You notice ducks tend to hang out in ponds with other ducks and chickens in a chicken coop with other chickens. Unless you live on a farm or work in or visit a zoo, rarely do you witness a flock of geese, ducks, and chickens assembled together.

However, this quote applies to people as well. People with similar likes, appearances, or behaviors tend to hang out together or associate with each other. However, if you explore this idea somewhat further, you will find that the more you associate with certain people, the more their likes, appearances, or behaviors assimilate into yours. Therefore, make a conscious effort to hang out with people of positive influence.

The Scriptures above allude to this point. 1 Corinthians 15:33 says, "Do not be deceived: 'Bad company corrupts good morals,'" and Galatians 5:9 says, "A little leaven leavens the whole lump of dough."

Pay attention to the company you keep. Carefully monitor who you associate, chill, hang, or spend time with so that you remain in step with the Lord. This will prevent you from reverting back to crawling again and keep you walking forward with the Lord.

Cultivate positive relationships. Do not be deceived by ungodly associations. It only takes a little bit of negative influence to ruin your thoughts, attitudes, and actions.

Discussion Points

1. Who are the people in your life that you spend a lot of time with? Why?

_____

_____

_____

2. What does "A little leaven leavens the whole lump of dough" mean?

_____

_____

_____

3. What kind of people do you need to avoid? Why?

_____

_____

_____

My Cu*fe* Daughter

_____

_____

_____

_____

_____

_____

_____

_____

_____

_____

_____

Covered Until The End

A Valued Treasure
Respect and Value

"But you are a chosen race, a royal priesthood, a holy nation, a people for God's own possession, so that you may proclaim the excellencies of Him who has called you out of darkness into His marvelous light…"
1 Peter 2:9

Imagine walking around in a department store, and you find yourself surrounded by very delicate and expensive glassware. Add a child to the picture. As you walk through the aisles of the store, you grasp the child's hand and gently explain why he or she must not touch or run around. You show the child the valuable items, the high prices the owner paid for them, and why he or she should not mishandle or break them.

You are fearfully and wonderfully made, a treasure respected and valued. Do not allow the men of this world who do not see your value or worth to touch or mishandle you. Men who desire to use, confuse, abuse and then lose you lack the knowledge of your royalty.

Your owner reflects your value. Jesus Christ paid the highest price for you—His life. He does not want His expensive piece of art to get mishandled, shattered, or broken. He wants you to receive respect and value because of whom you belong to. You represent royalty—God's chosen daughter!

Discussion Points

1. Have you ever broken something valuable? How did you feel? How do you think God feels when someone devalues you?

   _____

   _____

   _____

2. Name some things said or done that indicate someone does not value you.

   _____

   _____

   _____

3. What can you do when someone devalues you?

   _____

   _____

   _____

My Cu†e Daughter

_____

_____

_____

_____

_____

_____

_____

_____

_____

_____

_____

Covered Until The End

Watch What You Think
Your Thoughts

"We are destroying speculations and every lofty thing raised up against the knowledge of God, and we are taking every thought captive to the obedience of Christ..."
2 Corinthians 10:5

The mind holds the secret to successful living. So, who controls your mind? If you give Satan power over your mind, he keeps you leveled to the ground and in bondage with lies. You think you stand defeated; therefore, you talk, walk, and live a defeated life. You bring into existence the truth of a familiar saying, "A mind is a terrible thing to waste."

But if God's truth controls your mind, then you will soar in this life and live victoriously. God desires to free you from the chains that hold you hostage. He wants you to blossom into all that He created you to be. He wants you to remember that you are more than a conqueror!

A lot of people want someone else to think for them. Think for yourself. You become what you think. What lies in your heart penetrates your mind. Let the Word of God control your thinking. If something else controls it, reprogram your thinking. Remove the false data, and implant the truth.

But you must accept the renovations to bring about the changes. Jesus must tear down the old to bring in the new. It may take work, and it may feel painful as you adjust to new information because old habits prove hard to break. But the process is worth the effort if you really want to soar.

How can you do it? 2 Corinthians 10:5 tells us to take "every thought captive to the obedience of Christ." Every time you think something contrary to the Word of God, grab that thought, and take it hostage. Refuse to allow Satan to get a stronghold and create a wall in your mind that causes you to lose God's truth.

So if I ask, "Are You **Cu†e**?" what would you say? Well, if you think you are **Cu†e**, then you will emulate **Cu†e**. You will talk, walk, and live like a "fearfully and wonderfully made" daughter of the King!

Discussion Points

1. What does it mean, "We become what we think"?

    _____

    _____

    _____

2. What does it mean to grab a thought and take it hostage? Give an example.

    _____

    _____

    _____

3. What ways can you reprogram or remove false data in your mind about you?

    _____

    _____

    _____

My Cu⸁e Daughter

_____

_____

_____

_____

_____

_____

_____

_____

_____

_____

_____

Covered Until The End

A Person of Character
Integrity-Ethical-Honesty

"O Lord, who may abide in Your tent?
Who may dwell on Your holy hill?
He who walks with integrity, and works righteousness,
And speaks truth in his heart."
Psalm 15:1-2

"He leads the humble in justice,
And He teaches the humble His way.
All the paths of the Lord are lovingkindness and truth,
To those who keep His covenant and His testimonies."
Psalm 25:9-10

People often use three words interchangeably to describe one's character, and those three words are integrity, ethics, and honesty. They represent a system of moral values and how well a person adheres to them. There is a saying: "Sow a thought, reap an act. Sow an act, reap a habit. Sow a habit, reap your character. Sow your character, reap your destiny." Your character development starts with your thoughts, which lead to actions, which lead to habits. Your habits dictate your character, which affects your destiny.

Do you possess the qualities of truthfulness and honesty or do others know you for lying, cheating, and stealing? When faced with a moral decision, do you compromise because it feels better or because you wish to maintain your popularity status? Do you struggle with making decisions that require doing the right thing even if it means losing a friend or close relationship with someone?

It takes courage to distinguish yourself and stand up for what is right. Honest and ethical people do just that. People with integrity live authentically. They represent a rare breed of humanity that refuses to succumb to fear. They take risks for what they believe. Others look up to them for striving to model excellence in their behavior instead of practicing deception. Others point to them, watch them, respect them, admire them. Why? Because they tell the truth even if it hurts.

A consistent godly life represents an act of worship. Making a decision to stand for God means sometimes standing alone. You must stay humble so He can lead you to make the right choice. But choosing right will win every time. It gets easier the more you choose the right way.

Do you know people who appear to know what to do in any situation? They don't engage in long conversations, discussions, consultations, or meetings over issues. They just do what comes naturally from habit. Good habits allow you to respond quickly to situations without a lot of hesitation and deliberations. You know what God wants you to do because it's in His Word, and you do it. No second guessing, no making excuses.

Live differently. Practice truthfulness and honesty. Your uniqueness just may impact your school, place of work, neighborhood, or any of your spheres of influence. Remember, one person of truth can impact the entire world—that's what Jesus did!

Discussion Points

1. Give an example of what the saying in today's lesson means: "Sow a thought, reap an act..."

   _____

   _____

   _____

2. Think back on a time when you made a decision between doing right or wrong. What did you do? How did you feel? What was the outcome?

   _____

   _____

   _____

3. If people described you, what do you think they would say about your character? Why? If needed, what can you do to improve your character?

   _____

   _____

   _____

My Cu†e Daughter

_____

_____

_____

_____

_____

_____

_____

_____

_____

_____

Covered Until The End

The Gift of Imagination

Dreams or Goals

"The thief comes only to steal and kill and destroy; I came that they may have life, and have it abundantly."
John 10:10

What dreams stir your heart? Not your thoughts or images that occur while sleeping, but the plans or goals that God gives you. There's nothing wrong with pursuing career goals, but what goals do you hold in your heart that glorify the Lord, build up His kingdom, or minister to His people?

God gives you specific, personal, and intimate dreams. Others may view them as illogical or shocking. Your goals may sound crazy to them, and they may stare at you when you share them. They probably will appear unreachable by human standards, and they usually exist outside of your skill set or training. But the dreams or goals God gives you, will evoke a strong desire to accomplish them even when you don't know how to pull them off.

God gave you a wonderful gift called your imagination to help fuel dreams and goals. He wants you to imagine them, believe them, and achieve them. But it takes faith and determination to follow your dreams and goals. Imagination gets you going and propels you into your future. But if you only choose to live by sight and not by faith, you will miss out on all that He wants you to accomplish.

Go ahead—in your imagination, cross the bridge before you get to it. Don't let anyone kill, steal, or destroy your dreams or goals. Jesus came to give you abundant life. Imagine big, dream big, and do big things for the Lord. Visualize it, pray about it, believe it, and go for it!

I once wrote a song that captures this in the best way I know how.

> Imagination is the place, where hopes and dreams begin;
> It reaches far and stretches wide, a bridge that has no end.
> A passport to your future, a glimpse of who you can be;
> A chance to see the things that unbelieving eyes can't see.
>
> Chorus:
> I expect great things to happen, think big about what I can do;
> Create dreams in my mind, and with my heart I will follow through.
> Never folding up, holding up, never giving in;
> I can imagine… I will believe… and I know I will achieve.
> I'm determined to believe… I'm determined to believe.
>
> The biggest challenge you must face, will not be to achieve;
> You must see where you want to be, and then you must believe.
> Step by step, you'll get there, if you keep moving on;
> You'll find or make a way and then your dream will have begun.

Discussion Points

1. Name some of your dreams or goals in life.

   _____

   _____

   _____

2. What must you do to accomplish them? Describe your plan of action.

   _____

   _____

   _____

3. How will your dreams and goals give God honor and glory?

   _____

   _____

   _____

My Cu†e Daughter

_____

_____

_____

_____

_____

_____

_____

_____

_____

_____

_____

Covered Until The End

The Right Crowd
Friendships

"He who walks with wise men will be wise,
But the companion of fools will suffer harm."
Proverbs 13:20

"A friend loves at all times,
And a brother is born for adversity."
Proverbs 17:17

"A man of too many friends comes to ruin,
But there is a friend who sticks closer than a brother."
Proverbs 18:24

Everybody you meet is not your friend. True friendships must cultivate or grow. You may possess many acquaintances, colleagues, associates, or even random people you interact with, but all those relationships don't necessarily equate to friendship. In fact, we should heed the warning in Proverbs 18:24 of having too many friends.

True friends love you at all times. They love you during the good and bad of life. They love you enough to tell you when you are wrong. Proverbs 27:6 tells us that "Faithful are the wounds of a friend, but deceitful are the kisses of an enemy." Faithful friends love you so much that they speak honestly to you about dangerous situations and people to avoid. They help point out traps blinding you. They point and steer you in the right direction. A friend's loving eye may detect pitfalls that you fail to see.

True friends also love you enough to encourage you when you get discouraged. They cheer you on as you strive to accomplish your goals and dreams. When you fall down, they pick you up, and push you to keep moving ahead. They laugh, cry, pray, and rejoice with you through life's ups and downs.

Carefully choose who you hang out with. Relationships can destroy your life or build it up. Running with the wrong crowd will only lead to wrong decisions and actions which lead to negative outcomes.

Avoid people who indulge in alcohol and drugs. Stay away from those whose lifestyles consist of stealing, lying, gossiping, cussing and using other unwholesome language or actions. If you run with them, before long, you'll wind up doing the same.

Instead, hang out with people who live healthy, productive, and godly lifestyles. Surround yourself with nice, hard-working, and honest people. Associate with folks who study the Word of God and know the right thing to do when confronted with life's situations.

Choose friends wisely, and choose wise friends. Choose friends who walk with the Lord and hold you accountable. Walk with and learn from them. Running with the right crowd results in positive outcomes.

Discussion Points

1. What does the statement mean: "A man of many friends comes to ruin"?

    _____

    _____

    _____

2. Name some traps and pitfalls that you may be blind to that a friend might see.

    _____

    _____

    _____

3. What does it mean to choose friends wisely and choose wise friends?

    _____

    _____

    _____

My Cu†e Daughter

_____

_____

_____

_____

_____

_____

_____

_____

_____

_____

_____

Covered Until The End

Be Creative
Creativity

"In the beginning, God created the heavens and the earth."
Genesis 1:1

Genesis 1:1 says that in the beginning, God created. Look around and see what God did. Look at the oceans, landscapes, animals, plants, and humans. His signature rests on everything. We enjoy the beauty and majesty of His creation without really understanding all the intricacies, complexities, and details.

God loves creativity and even though His character remains the same, His methods and ways to accomplish His purposes change. He alters things and uses so many unpredictable ways to bring about freshness and newness.

God made us in His image and instilled in us a desire to create. He wanted us to use our inventiveness to produce or make things with our imagination. Our creations should be beneficial to mankind and give Him glory.

Creativity brings freshness and change. To be creative, you must remain open to new things, willing to change your thinking, and ready to introduce or begin something unfamiliar.

Discussion Points

1. How do you see God's creativity in mankind?

   _____

   _____

   _____

2. Name some things that you have created. How do they benefit others and glorify the Lord?

   _____

   _____

   _____

3. What things do you need to remain open to so that you are more creative?

   _____

   _____

   _____

My Cu†e Daughter

_____

_____

_____

_____

_____

_____

_____

_____

_____

_____

_____

Covered Until The End

Ready to Share
Generosity, Hospitality and Kindness

"Instruct them to do good, to be rich in good works, to be generous and ready to share…"
1 Timothy 6:18

"Be hospitable to one another without complaint. As each one has received a special gift, employ it in serving one another, as good stewards of the manifold grace of God."
1 Peter 4:9-10

"Do not let kindness and truth leave you;
Bind them around your neck,
Write them on the tablet of your heart."
Proverbs 3:3

Reflect on God's gifts to you. Your family, home, food, clothes, health, education, mental stability, friends, special skills, and talents represent just a few of His many blessings. As you think about all that the Lord freely gave you, it should motivate you to freely give to others. God promises that if you sow bountifully, you will reap bountifully. So, give freely and liberally.

You can give generously with your time, money, or talents. Whether you take the time to listen to a hurting friend, write a check to donate to a needy cause, meet a financial need for someone, or help construct a prop for a play, God desires that you demonstrate generosity. By doing so, you display His love, and He takes delight in you.

The gift of hospitality offers a pleasant and warm environment. It involves making people feel welcomed, respected, important, and valuable. When you create a loving and friendly atmosphere, people experience warmth and the love of God that flows through you. Be cordial and readily receptive of others. Treat people as special guests and put them at ease.

Hospitality cleanses away selfishness and self-centeredness from your heart. You will feel better knowing you not only contributed to a need, but brought warmth and love to someone. These moments and feelings trigger the joy that always comes to those who practice hospitality.

Show kindness to people in words and deeds. Put helping others at the top of your list. When you extend kindness to others, you display consideration and sensitivity to their needs. Jesus cared for the physical, emotional, and spiritual needs of people. He equips us to do the same.

God gave His most valuable gift—His Son, Jesus Christ. Jesus unselfishly gave His life to give you eternal life. And what was the motivation? Love! Just model Jesus' love and continuous goodness to others.

Be a channel of blessing and share with God's people in need when you can. Do it without hesitation. Do it without complaining. Do it willingly. Do it with no remorse or reservation. Let your service prove evidence of the Holy Spirit's work in you.

Discussion Points

1. What does it mean to be "rich in good works"?

   _____

   _____

   _____

2. Name some ways you can share your gifts to help others.

   _____

   _____

   _____

3. How can you share God's most valuable gift to you?

   _____

   _____

   _____

My Cu†e Daughter

_____

_____

_____

_____

_____

_____

_____

_____

_____

_____

_____

Covered Until The End

47

A Servant's Heart
Servanthood

"Whatever you do, do your work heartily as for the Lord, rather than for men; knowing that from the Lord you will receive the reward of the inheritance. It is the Lord Christ whom you serve."
Colossians 3:23-24

"Therefore humble yourselves under the mighty hand of God, that He may exalt you at the proper time..."
1 Peter 5:6

The ability to help someone else brings great pleasure. When you go beyond yourself and lend a helping hand, you exhibit traits of a servant. A servant's heart represents someone who serves with a spirit of gratefulness. Someone who takes care of and ministers to the body of Christ. Someone who stands willing to step up without being asked. Someone who anticipates others' needs and strives to show love in action. Someone who epitomizes the heart of Mary Magdalene, one of the greatest servants to Jesus.

Sometimes those who serve faithfully in the body of Christ get tired or feel unrecognized. But remember, the Lord sees everything you do for Him; nothing goes unnoticed. He encourages us in 1 Peter 5:6 saying, "Humble yourselves under the mighty hand of God, that He may exalt you at the proper time." Whether recognition occurs on this side of heaven or not, rest assured that He will reward you in eternity. But those who serve well now deserve a pat on the back for a job well done.

Many examples of servanthood exist in the Bible, but the greatest example came in the form of deity, Jesus, who humbled Himself to wash His disciples' feet. But His love in action went deeper. Jesus willingly went to the cross to meet our need for salvation and reconciliation to God. Yet, far too often, we fail to give Him the recognition He so richly deserves.

Instead of looking for and expecting recognition from others here on earth, focus on ministering with a servant's heart for Him. If you do, He will exalt you in the proper time.

Discussion Points

1. What did Mary Magdalene do in Matthew 26:6-13 to show servanthood?

_____

_____

_____

2. Who do you know with a servant's heart that you would like to emulate? Why?

_____

_____

_____

3. How can you go beyond yourself and lend a helping hand?

_____

_____

_____

My Cu*te* Daughter

_____
_____
_____
_____
_____
_____
_____
_____
_____
_____
_____
_____

Covered Until The End

A Wonderful Love

God's View of You

"For God so loved the world, that He gave His only begotten Son, that whoever believes in Him shall not perish, but have eternal life."
John 3:16

"For whom He foreknew, He also predestined to become conformed to the image of His Son, so that He would be the firstborn among many brethren…"
Romans 8:29

The movie *Wonder* tells the inspiring and heartfelt story of a little boy named August Pullman. August suffered from Treacher Collins syndrome, a rare genetic disorder caused by an anomaly in his DNA characterized by facial deformities of the ears, eyes, cheekbones, and chin.

August's parents loved him fiercely and desired desperately to protect him. Due to numerous surgeries, his mom homeschooled him. But as he approached middle school age, his parents decided to enroll him in private school. He entered the fifth grade attending a mainstream elementary school for the first time.

Initially, nearly the entire student body ostracized him, but later on, one of his classmates befriended him. His parents' hearts ached for his anguish and rejoiced in his successes as he navigated his way in the world of the 5th grade.

The story touched on kindness, compassion, and friendship. It addressed the importance of acceptance and trying to fit in. It highlighted the current climate of bullying that still exists today. It also demonstrated how negative and bias attitudes pass from one generation to another.

In one touching scene filled with lots of emotion and frustration, August told his dad that he must be ashamed of him every time his dad looked at his face. His dad cupped his face in his hand, looked August straight in the eye and said, "I know you don't always like it, but I love it. It's my son's face."

What a love—a wonderful love!

It represents the kind of love God shares with us. God the Father loves Jesus fiercely. We receive that same love when we accept Jesus as our Lord and Savior. God desires desperately to protect us and His heart aches for our anguish and rejoices in our successes as we navigate our way in the world of life. He endures His children's pain. And no matter what the world says about your looks, God cups your face and looks you straight in the eye and says, "I know you don't always like it, but I love it. It's my Son's face."

You see, when God looks at you and me, He sees Jesus' atonement which covers our deformities and sin! The blood of Jesus covers us. Oh, what a wonder—a wonderful love!

Discussion Points

1. How do you think a person feels when they suffer from any deformity?

   _____

   _____

   _____

2. What can you do to show Jesus' love to that person?

   _____

   _____

   _____

3. If you are His child by accepting Jesus as your Lord and Savior, why does God see Jesus when He looks at you?

   _____

   _____

   _____

My Cu†e Daughter

_____

_____

_____

_____

_____

_____

_____

_____

_____

_____

_____

Covered Until The End

Make Wise Decisions
Decision Making & Wisdom

"If it is disagreeable in your sight to serve the Lord, choose for yourselves today whom you will serve…but as for me and my house, we will serve the Lord."
Joshua 24:15

*"The fear of the Lord is the beginning of wisdom,
And the knowledge of the Holy One is understanding."*
Proverbs 9:10

Every decision you make in life will produce a result. Good decisions will result in successful outcomes, and poor decisions lead to sometimes serious and long-lasting negative consequences. Learn to make wise choices. Choose well from all the possibilities affecting your decision.

How do you make wise decisions? Wisdom comes from respecting God and His Word, and knowing how to use His Word when faced with life decisions. The book of Proverbs lists many benefits to acquiring wisdom which gives you the ability to live all areas of your life skillfully. In fact, Proverbs 8:11a says, "For wisdom is better than jewels." Proverbs 9:10 reminds us that "The fear of the Lord is the beginning of wisdom, and the knowledge of the Holy One is understanding."

James 1:5 says, "But if any of you lacks wisdom, let him ask of God, who gives to all generously and without reproach, and it will be given to him." Bring God's Word into every decision you make. He welcomes decisions regarding your education, work, marriage, children, house, money, and even decisions that seem trivial or insignificant. Simply ask Him what you should do. He promised to give you the answer. It may not be the one you wanted or expected, but it will be the one that puts you on the right path.

You've probably heard the saying "There are two things in this world that you have got to do: die and pay your taxes." See, when the federal income tax due date arrives each year, many people fall short of paying their taxes. While options exist to pay off the debt, the choice to pay still remains. You even get a warning about what will happen if you rebel and refuse to pay. Consequences range from mounting debt to jail time. These repercussions can disrupt your life for a while, but you can still recover.

However, one day you will face the most important decision of your life. It will be the one thing you've "got to do." You must decide where you will spend eternity. An event will come that you cannot recover from—death. You will die and leave this earth, either on your appointed due date or you will be raptured at Jesus' second coming. Once you breathe your last breath, you will go to heaven or hell. If you choose to rebel against accepting God's plan of salvation, you choose eternal death. If you accept Jesus Christ, you choose eternal life.

Study God's Word daily and use it to make wise decisions. You will enjoy a long, productive, and successful life. Proverbs 8:35 assures, "For he who finds [wisdom] finds life, and obtains favor from the Lord."

Discussion Points

1. How do you acquire wisdom? Name some benefits to possessing wisdom.

   _____

   _____

   _____

2. Why is "wisdom better than jewels"?

   _____

   _____

   _____

3. What is the most important decision you will ever make in life? Why? Name some decisions that seem trivial or insignificant. What do you do with these?

   _____

   _____

   _____

My Cu*te* Daughter

_____

_____

_____

_____

_____

_____

_____

_____

_____

_____

_____

Covered Until The End

Leap of Faith
Risk Taking

"And He said to them, 'Why are you afraid? Do you still have no faith?'"
Mark 4:40

One of my favorite excursions on any vacation involves an ATV (All-Terrain Vehicle) adventure. On one of our trips to Hawaii, my husband and I went to explore Kauai's Kipu Ranch on a 4-hour waterfalls and picnic tour with unique and challenging terrain leading through cool forest roads, lush green pastures to mountainside trails. We enjoyed beautiful views, incredible wildlife, historical sites, and even some movie locations.

One of our stopping points landed us along the Hule'ia River to the "Indiana Jones Swing." Yes, the famous swing scene easily recalled by those who watched the movie. The swing represented danger, anticipation, excitement, and adventure. Was Indy going to risk it? Would the rope hold his weight? Would the waters below provide safety for his landing? Would he take the leap of faith?

We faced the same question. Our guide offered us a chance to take the Indy swing. He provided instructions and safety tips. He gave us a choice to take the risk, grab the rope, swing out, and swing back in if we didn't want to take the plunge into the river.

Well, I love a challenge, but quite honestly, I pondered this a bit despite my excitement. Not because of the water since I swim well. Usually heights pose hesitancy, but the rope's position hung within my height standards. I got ready to go but hesitated because no other adult immediately jumped at the opportunity.

Of course, the children took the leap. I watched as they jumped with excitement in their eyes. Finally, one woman answered the call. I couldn't stand it any longer and decided to take the risk. I decided to take the leap of faith. I grabbed the rope, swung out, let go and plunged into the river. I felt the excitement of doing something new and refreshing. Guess what? I did it again!

Learn to take some risks. Some may result in pain, but you will learn valuable lessons and grow into the person God designed you to be. We miss out on the adventures of life God presents us because we fear the unknown or lack the faith that keeps us from grabbing the ropes and swinging into new and refreshing beginnings. Sometimes we miss the chance thinking *I'll do it next time or later*—yet, later never comes.

So, grab the ropes, swing ahead, and take the leap of faith. You may find yourself refreshed. Go into deep waters. Go out on a limb. Remember Zacchaeus climbed out on a limb before he saw Jesus (Luke 19:1-10). Sometimes we must take a risk before we see Him too.

Discussion Points

1. Give an example of a risk you took? What was the result?

   _____

   _____

   _____

2. What adventure did you miss out on because you failed to take a leap of faith?

   _____

   _____

   _____

3. What is the meaning of "Sometimes we must take a risk before we see Him"?

   _____

   _____

   _____

My Cu†e Daughter

_____

_____

_____

_____

_____

_____

_____

_____

_____

_____

_____

Covered Until The End

Jesus, Take the Wheel

Guidance

"For such is God,
Our God forever and ever;
He will guide us until death."
Psalm 48:14

"I will lead the blind by a way they do not know,
In paths they do not know I will guide them.
I will make darkness into light before them
And rugged places into plains.
These are the things I will do,
And I will not leave them undone."
Isaiah 42:16

The singer Carrie Underwood rose to fame in 2005 as the winner of the fourth season of American Idol. One of her singles, *Jesus, Take the Wheel*, became a huge success. The lyrics of the song emphasized how much we need to relinquish control to the Lord.

We tend to think we lose control if we give it to Him. *What if Jesus wants me to do something I don't want to do or go someplace I don't want to go? If I give Jesus full control of my life, then that means I must hand over the steering wheel to Him.*

Talk about fear seeping into your heart. Talk about a true test of faith. But consider who gets the wheel. Jesus reigns King of Kings and Lord of Lords. He created you with a plan for your life from beginning to end.

His eternal perspective and character allow us to trust Him. His infinite and perfect knowledge assures us that He will drive us in the right direction and never steer us down a wrong path. His indescribable love for us propels Him to work out all things for our good (Romans 8:28).

God speaks His instructions through His Word—the Bible. But we must read, accept, and apply them. However, we quite often just don't want to give up the wheel. But no matter how much He desires to sit in the driver's seat, Jesus will not force you to give Him the wheel. You must, despite your fears, willingly give it to Him. Once you do, you can sit back, relax, and enjoy the ride. Remember, He promised to cover you until the end.

Who do you think represents the better driver of your life? Do you possess credentials better than His? Learn to daily leave the driving to Him. He will guide you safely to your destination in life. When faced with difficult situations, cry out, "Jesus, Take the Wheel."

Discussion Points

1. Why is this statement erroneous: "I lose control if I give Him control"?

_____

_____

_____

2. Why do you think we hesitate to accept Jesus' guidance?

_____

_____

_____

3. What area of your life do you find difficult giving control over to Jesus?

_____

_____

_____

My Cu†e Daughter

_____

_____

_____

_____

_____

_____

_____

_____

_____

_____

_____

_____

Covered Until The End

Follow to Lead

Leadership

"How blessed are those whose way is blameless,
Who walk in the law of the Lord.
How blessed are those who observe His testimonies,
Who seek Him with all their heart."
Psalm 119:1-2

"O send out Your light and Your truth, let them lead me;
Let them bring me to Your holy hill
And to Your dwelling places."
Psalm 43:3

Many people strive to lead. But what does it take to be a great and effective leader? Why do people tend to easily follow someone? What distinguishes that person from another? It all boils down to the person's character. Effective leaders possess personal qualities and characteristics that attract people to follow them. How did they develop these qualities? They learned to be great followers.

What do I mean? To develop into a great leader, you must first exhibit traits of a good follower. The person you follow should possess the characteristics that shape a godly character. The perfect candidate is Jesus Christ. You must first follow Jesus to develop the traits of effective godly leadership. These traits exist in God's Word. Traits such as love, caring about others, commitment, competence, integrity, honesty, servanthood, courage, effective communication, discipline, vision, passion, and many others contribute to one's overall character.

Studying God's Word and doing things His way will ensure that you develop the character of Jesus. The process takes time. You must stay close to the heart of God. Since Jesus stands as the greatest leader, following Him will guarantee leadership success. He will develop you from the inside out and empower you to eventually lead others to good and righteous endeavors.

There will come times as a leader when you need to step aside. Everyone lacks certain necessary skills, so don't expect to lead every aspect of an assignment or project. During your development process, you will discover your unique skills and abilities as well as your weaknesses. Let others who possess the skills you lack take the lead in their area of expertise. Show them that you care and value their abilities.

Jesus' character revolves around His love and care for us. The character of an effective leader should revolve around the love and care of others. People find it easy to follow someone who cares about them. As John Maxwell, an expert on godly leadership stated, "People don't care how much you know, until they know how much you care."

Follow those who exhibit effective leadership qualities that result in godly character. Lead with a heart that's molded from the inside out. To become the leader that people want to follow, keep growing in God's Word.

Discussion Points

1. What traits would make people want to follow you?

   _____

   _____

   _____

2. What traits do you need to work on to become an effective and godly leader? How will you develop them?

   _____

   _____

   _____

3. What does John Maxwell's statement mean: "People don't care how much you know, until they know how much you care"? As a leader, how can you show someone you care?

   _____

   _____

   _____

My Cu*t*e Daughter

_____

_____

_____

_____

_____

_____

_____

_____

_____

_____

_____

Covered Until The End

Cherish Your Body
Sexual Purity

"Do you not know that your bodies are members of Christ? Shall I then take away the members of Christ and make them members of a prostitute? May it never be!"
1 Corinthians 6:15

"Flee immorality. Every other sin that a man commits is outside the body, but the immoral man sins against his own body. Or do you not know that your body is a temple of the Holy Spirit who is in you, whom you have from God, and that you are not your own? For you have been bought with a price: therefore glorify God in your body"
1 Corinthians 6:18-20

We live in a sex-craved world where the motto shouts, "It's your thing; do what you want to do." But don't let the crowd dictate what you know goes against God's Word. God places a very high value on sexual purity. Since He created sex, He gets to set the standards governing it.

God created sex for procreation to expand His image on earth. He also created it as enjoyment in the marriage relationship. God blessed intimacy between husband and wife. Remember everything that He created was good. God designed the gift of sex for human fulfilment. It represents a legitimate passion to be enjoyed in a legitimate way.

Because God values sexual purity, He wants you committed to chastity before marriage. He wants you to use your body to glorify Him. Remember your body is a member of Christ, so when you join your body sexually with someone else outside of marriage, you take Christ with you. Will Jesus enjoy this union?

The only legitimate and biblical use of sex resides within marriage. In the context of marriage, a man and woman commit to each other and become one. No guilt or shame results. The husband and wife experience warmth and love, and Christ joyfully approves this union.

Sexual activity outside of marriage constitutes a sin. If you fall into this sin, you can receive forgiveness and rededicate yourself to Christ. But keep in mind that immorality does tremendous damage to your soul. Even though God forgives you once you truly repent, forgiving yourself takes longer. The scars left from illegitimate relationships leave long-lasting results.

The Lord called you to sanctification and sexual purity. Guard your sexual purity. The Bible says to "flee immorality." Protect your eyes and ears from immoral things which can stir up sin. When temptation presents itself, walk away or run. Don't place yourself in environments that tempt you to fall.

Guarding your sexual purity will cost you. You may come across as "uppity" or boring. You may not fit in with the crowd. You may lose so-called friends and feel alone. But God will honor your dedication to Him. Follow His design. He will reward you for your faithfulness. The reward will always prove greater than the cost.

Discussion Points

1. Some compare sex outside of marriage to a fire outside of the fireplace? What does the analogy mean?

2. What does it mean to guard your sexual purity? What things can you do when faced with this temptation?

3. Name some other costs you may experience. Name some of the rewards of guarding your sexual purity.

My Cu†e Daughter

Covered Until The End

A Love Letter

True Love

"Love is patient, love is kind and is not jealous; love does not brag and is not arrogant, does not act unbecomingly; it does not seek its own, is not provoked, does not take into account a wrong suffered, does not rejoice in unrighteousness, but rejoices with the truth; bears all things, believes all things, hopes all things, endures all things. Love never fails…"
1 Corinthians 13:4-8a

(Enter the recipient's name in the blanks.)

Dear _____, I love you so deeply. Words fail to express my deep affection and devotion to you. Your beauty takes my breath away and no one else comes close to your uniqueness. You compare to a fine, wonderfully built brick house, and I delight in the fact that you belong to me! Our union together and all that we shall endure over the years cause me to love you more.

Because I love you so much, I will remain patient and kind with you, never resenting you for things you accomplish or possess. I desire the best for you. Even when we disagree, and I prove to be right, no record or list of wins and losses exists. You are so special to me that I refuse to allow anger to surface and if it does, the anger is short-lived.

I delight and rejoice in you and me and our union. I will always protect and defend you, _____. I realize you hold dreams and goals, and I hope you know that I stand beside you in helping you accomplish the desires of your heart. Never doubt my love for you. Continue to believe in me and our love. Please know that you can completely trust me.

The vow I made to you ensures we remain together. Therefore, I persevere with you helping you overcome any difficulties you face. I promise never to fail you. I love you, _____, more than you will ever realize.

I love you to death. You remain mine forever.

Contemplate the words written in this expression of love for you. The declarations affirm your worth and value. Nourish them by reading certain parts over and over again.

Where did the letter come from? Well, even though I wrote this letter as an example, it mimics the ideas found in a real letter—the Bible, God's love letter to you. He created you with a need for love, but without Him, love proves nonexistent because Jesus is love.

As much as any man can love you, his love sometimes fails to do everything he promises. But everything Jesus promises to do, He can and will do it. He's the only man who actually loved you to death—death upon the cross.

Jesus understands our need for love, which really translates into a desperate need for Him. Read His love letter constantly, and get ready to fall in love with Him all over again. Instead of focusing on flowers, candy, jewelry, or other tokens of temporary love, cherish His eternal love.

Discussion Points

1. How do the words in the letter make you feel?

    _____

    _____

    _____

2. What parts of the love letter do you really like? Why?

    _____

    _____

    _____

3. How can you show Jesus that you love Him?

    _____

    _____

    _____

My Cuｷe Daughter

_____

_____

_____

_____

_____

_____

_____

_____

_____

_____

_____

Covered Until The End

Be Adaptable
Flexibility

"To the weak, I became weak, that I might win the weak; I have become all things to all men, so that I may by all means save some."
1 Corinthians 9:22

"I know how to get along with humble means, and I also know how to live in prosperity; in any and every circumstance I have learned the secret of being filled and going hungry, both of having abundance and suffering need."
Philippians 4:12

Your willingness to bend or adjust to change reflects your flexibility and adaptability. People who remain open-minded and receptive to new ideas make a difference. People who fight for their own agenda and remain self-centered become stiff and inflexible both in their relationship with Christ and others.

If you possess an attitude that resists change, you will miss out on new opportunities to grow. These attitudes usually reside in people who hold fast to long-held rituals or behaviors, people who run away from new or different ideas, people suspicious of the unfamiliar, and people who just plain despise change. They yield to the familiar and resist openness to innovation.

Flexibility involves your response and attitude towards changes. You've heard the saying, "There are two sides to every coin." Almost everything presents two sides. If you desire to grow and experience greater heights, yield to the side of openness. Don't settle so strongly in your opinions that you neglect to consider the other side. Allow room for newness. Remove the "Do not disturb sign" and open the door of your heart to the untried and unexpected.

I must stress one caveat: while staying open to the ideas and suggestions of others, remember to hold on to the truth of God's Word. Never waver or change what He says. Remain wise as you accept insights from others. Ask the Lord for guidance and wisdom to accept something new. He will give it to you.

God fills our hearts with new changes and goals. He may ask you to move to a different city, state, or country. He may not ask you to move at all, but simply to do something totally unexpected. He may ask you to spend time with someone entirely different from you. He just desires your willingness to do it. Be flexible. Adapt and embrace new ways, new ideas, new friendships, and enjoy new opportunities to grow.

Discussion Points

1. How do you feel about change? When have you exhibited flexibility and adaptability? What did Paul mean by, "To the weak, I became weak, that I might win the weak; I have become all things to all men, so that I may by all means save some"?

   _____

   _____

   _____

2. Why do you think people put up the "Do not disturb" sign when it comes to change?

   _____

   _____

   _____

3. What does it mean to remember to hold on to the truth of God's Word? Give an example of when we should not adjust or change something related to God's Word.

   _____

   _____

   _____

My Cu*f*e Daughter

_____

_____

_____

_____

_____

_____

_____

_____

_____

_____

_____

Covered Until The End

65

Noah Says No
Saying Yes

"And we know that God causes all things to work together for good to those who love God, to those who are called according to His purpose."
Romans 8:28

When my little granddaughter Noah turned two years old, we encountered the stage where her response to almost everything echoed NO! She would say "NO," even when she sometimes meant yes. She said "NO," to things beneficial to her. She said "NO," because she didn't believe or trust you. It never mattered whether she really understood. She usually responded "NO," since she learned to say it so well.

"Do you want the lollipop?"

"NO," when she really meant "yes" because she loved lollipops.

"Eat some more food, Noah."

"NO," even though she beckoned for another chicken nugget.

"Jump in my arms, Noah."

"NO," because she didn't trust that I would catch her the first time I asked her.

"Do you know how beautiful you are, Noah?"

"NO," because she didn't understand the essence of what I said, and she only knew "NO."

As I started thinking of Noah's responses, a question came to mind: How many times a day do we, as daughters of the King, say "NO" to Him?

Do we say "NO," even when it appears beneficial for us? He did promise that He "causes all things to work together for good to those who love God, to those who are called according to His purpose" (Romans 8:28). Do we say "NO," when He asks us to walk into the plan that He prepared for us simply because we run scared and don't trust Him? Do we say "NO," when He tells us that we are "fearfully and wonderfully made" because we simply refuse to believe that His Word represents truth? Do we say "NO," because like Noah, we too learned to say it so well?

We say "NO," to the Lord so many times by our words and actions. Maybe, like Noah, we need to be introduced to other words. "Yes, Lord, I believe that I am fearfully and wonderfully made and I will act like the beautiful masterpiece You designed. Yes, Lord, I will trust You even when I don't understand or it doesn't make sense. Yes, Lord, I will do it even though it may not feel good, but I believe it will all work together for good."

Discussion Points

1. What are some areas in which you have responded "NO" to God?

    _____

    _____

    _____

2. What prevents you from saying "yes"?

    _____

    _____

    _____

3. What does this verse mean: "And we know that God causes all things to work together for good to those who love God, to those who are called according to His purpose"?

    _____

    _____

    _____

My Cu†e Daughter

_____

_____

_____

_____

_____

_____

_____

_____

_____

_____

Covered Until The End

67

Are We There Yet?

Patience on the Journey

"Be anxious for nothing, but in everything by prayer and supplication with thanksgiving let your requests be made known to God. And the peace of God, which surpasses all comprehension, will guard your hearts and your minds in Christ Jesus."
Philippians 4:6-7

Are we there yet? This is a familiar phrase for anyone bold enough to take children on a road trip. I know this nerve-racking adventure all too well. When our sons were younger, we lived in Florida. All of our immediate family lived in South Carolina. We took trips to see them once or twice a year. Even though the boys got familiar with the ride, it didn't matter. We still heard those nerve-racking words, "Mom, Dad, are we there yet?"

"No, not quite."

Thirty minutes later: "Are we there yet?"

"No, we'll let you know."

Thirty minutes later: "Branden's touching me. Are we there yet?"

"No, we are not. I told you we'd let you know, and Branden, stop touching your brother."

An hour later: "Ryan is looking at me. Are we there yet?"

"Okay, that's it. No more questions. Just sit back, be quiet, and enjoy the ride. Ryan, don't look at Branden. Branden, don't touch Ryan. Both of you look out of your windows, and keep your hands to yourself!"

As nerve-racking as the conversation grew, I believed they kept asking the question "Are we there yet?" because they were so excited about the trip and seeing their grandparents, aunts, uncles, and cousins. I wonder do we get so excited about the journey the Lord has prepared for us that we ask Him, "Lord, are we there yet?"

It may seem that it's taking us a long time to get where He wants us to go. Maybe we get anxious and impatient because we envision too many stops and detours along the way. Maybe we just don't trust Him or trust that He will let us know when we arrive.

Does your journey bring excitement? Do you eagerly anticipate who you will see and meet along the way? Do you savor what's prepared for your arrival upon reaching your destination?

Want to know the secret to a worry-free journey? Let God do the driving. He already designed the map. He knows the roads to take. He knows how long the trip will last. He knows the best route for you even with the stops and detours along the way. Remain patient. He knows when you will arrive at your destination. He just wants you to trust Him. His timing is perfect! So, buckle up, sit back, relax, and enjoy the ride!

Discussion Points

1. Think of a time when you took a road trip? How did you feel? Why?

_____

_____

_____

2. What prevents you from getting excited about your journey?

_____

_____

_____

3. How can you reduce any anxiety or remain patient while on the journey? What does today's Scripture tell you to do?

_____

_____

_____

My Cu†e Daughter

_____

_____

_____

_____

_____

_____

_____

_____

_____

_____

_____

_____

Covered Until The End

The Price of Image

Image

"God created man in His own image, in the image of God He created him; male and female He created them."
Genesis 1:27

"Do nothing from selfishness or empty conceit, but with humility of mind regard one another as more important than yourselves…"
Philippians 2:3

I enjoy watching the Winter Olympics. It's amazing to watch the athletes compete, and even if they fail to win the gold, silver, or bronze medal, I applaud them for representing the best of the best. I particularly remember the 1994 Winter Olympics and the sad drama that occurred between Nancy Kerrigan and Tonya Harding.

Tonya skated gracefully. Her guts and determination made her a fierce competitor. She could consistently land the triple axel—one of the toughest figure skating jumps. It set her apart and opened the door for so many possibilities. However, she lost focus on her gifts. Instead, she started focusing on her looks and appearance—her image.

You see, the figure skating world wanted the image of an "ice princess." Dorothy Hamill possessed the image. Nancy Kerrigan inherited the image. But Tonya Harding lacked it. People viewed her as the "ugly duckling" with frizzy blonde hair from the other side of the tracks. She would never fit the beauty mold. She would never own that image.

Tonya could have won the Olympic title simply by doing what God designed her to do—skate like a world-class figure skater. But Tonya wanted the publicity and attention. She coveted Dorothy and Nancy's image, and this drove her to conspire and organize the vicious attack on Nancy Kerrigan. Tonya received probation, community service, and a hefty fine. The Olympics organization stripped her medals, forced her to withdraw from the World Figure Skating Championships, and banned her from other major competitions. Oh, the price of image!

Did Tonya get the publicity and attention? Yes, but not the kind she envisioned. People today remember her in a negative way. She paid a hefty price for an unclaimed image-—"ice princess."

The comparison trap drains you. It causes you to take desperate steps to emulate something other than what God intended. Constantly comparing yourself to others results in a self-defeating cycle. When you bump into someone on the street, at church, or anywhere who in your eyes represents the epitome of beauty, you feel defeated.

God gave you a divine gift to use for His glory, so stop comparing yourself to the world's standard of beauty. Avoid making foolish decisions to obtain "a particular image" which may result in negative attention and publicity. Just do what God designed you to do. Ask yourself, "What will the Lord say about me, His daughter?" Then decide if you want to pay the price for an image that does not reflect Him.

Discussion Points

1. What does the term image mean? What hefty price did Tonya Harding pay for trying to fit a certain image?

2. Name a time when you got caught up in the comparison trap. What does it mean to "Do nothing from selfishness or empty conceit"?

3. Name some things you can do when the comparison trap raises its ugly head.

My Cu†e Daughter

Stay in the Word

Read Scripture

"This book of the law shall not depart from your mouth, but you shall meditate on it day and night, so that you may be careful to do according to all that is written in it; for then you will make your way prosperous, and then you will have success."
Joshua 1:8

"All Scripture is inspired by God and profitable for teaching, for reproof, for correction, for training in righteousness; that the man of God may be adequate, equipped for every good work."
2 Timothy 3:16-17

Compare the Bible to a buffet of healthy foods eaten daily. It represents food for your soul and the more you eat, the healthier you become. Ingest God's Word eagerly and often. Savor it within your heart. It provides you with a balanced and healthy life and helps you to grow in the image of Jesus. Psalm 34:8 tells us to "taste and see that the Lord is good."

Reading the Bible gives you the proper perspective on issues in your life, whether they concern your family, friends, enemies, careers, money, etc. The Bible is the voice of God in print. The words in the pages speak of God's promises to you. You can count on the truth of His Word.

When faced with discouragement, molehills become mountains; small irritations emerge into volcanos; motivation and hope fade away. But God's Word transforms your thought process and brings new light into the picture. Reading the Scriptures provides encouragement and hope. They help you to persevere through your circumstances so you don't become despondent.

So, when life hits you hard with a disappointment or hurt and things get so bad that you just want to hit back—don't. Instead, hit the book! Open your Bible, and cling to God's Word. Whatever you struggle with, whatever you need, His Word covers you!

Clinging to His Word will help you avoid the tendency to react to situations based on your feelings. Instead, you will act according to the Word of God resulting in righteous behavior and a prosperous outcome.

However, the secret lies in applying the Word, not just reading it. James 1:22 says, "But prove yourselves doers of the word, and not merely hearers who delude themselves." It's easy to talk about doing what you read; it's harder actually doing what the Bible commands you to do.

We end up bloated with Scripture, but starved of action. Memorizing Scripture and consistently spending time studying His Word prove beneficial only if we apply His instructions. We will never go wrong. He will guide us to where we need to go.

God gave you His instructions for life. When He returns, He won't concern Himself with how many verses you memorized, how many Bible studies you attended, or how many sermons you listened to. He will only focus on what you did with His instructions!

So, begin each day with the Lord. Find a few moments of quiet time to read a portion of Scripture to seek guidance for the day. Eat from His menu. Chew on spiritual food. Act on His Word.

Discussion Points

1. What does "taste and see that the Lord is good" mean?

   _____

   _____

   _____

2. What does it mean to be "bloated with Scripture but starved of action"?

   _____

   _____

   _____

3. Give an example of reacting based on your feelings versus acting on God's Word.

   _____

   _____

   _____

My Cu*te Daughter

_____

_____

_____

_____

_____

_____

_____

_____

_____

_____

_____

Covered Until The End

Talk to Jesus

Pray

"Rejoice always; pray without ceasing; in everything give thanks; for this is God's will for you in Christ Jesus."
1 Thessalonians 5:16-18

"But certainly God has heard;
He has given heed to the voice of my prayer.
Blessed be God,
Who has not turned away my prayer
Nor His lovingkindness from me."
Psalm 66:19-20

An old familiar hymn by Cleavant Derricks goes like this:

Now let us have a little talk with Jesus,
let us tell Him all about our troubles,
He will hear our faintest cry,
and He will answer by and by
Now when you feel a little prayer wheel turning,
and you know a little fire is burning
You will find a little talk with Jesus makes it right.

As you journey through life, pray about everything. Pray daily. Pray without ceasing. Make prayer a consistent part of your daily activities. Consult the Lord on decisions for your entire life—your career, mate, children, friends, goals, dreams, and not just when things go wrong.

Talk to Jesus about what you desire out of life. Tell Him how you feel about things. Let Him know how you perceive you so that if your perception misaligns with His Word, He can guide you by the truth. Talk to Him about the desires of your heart. Indicate your dreams and goals. Talk about your failures, unmet expectations, and disappointments. The beauty lies in the fact that He already knows, and whatever you tell Him, stays with Him.

Jesus wants you to talk to Him daily. Ask for help when you need it. We all need help at times. Sometimes He sends people to assist you. They provide rich sources of information, knowledge, and advice. Sometimes the help lies in His Word.

You will face challenges and problems. Problems allow you to cry out and call on Jesus. Tell Him all about your troubles. Pray about how to solve them, and wait for His divine solutions. The best way will always point to His way. You remain in God's will and experience His peace. As long as you cry out to Jesus, you will see Him work for your good and His glory. He takes you to a deeper level of trust and belief in Him.

Talk to Jesus about everything! Nothing exists that you can't tell Him. He will not turn away your prayers. He listens to everything—your cries and pleas, your laughter and joy, tears and pain, your thankfulness and gratitude. As the song says, you will find a little talk with Jesus daily makes everything right!

Discussion Points

1. What does "pray without ceasing" mean? Does it mean we must kneel 24-hours a day and pray nonstop?

   _____

   _____

   _____

2. Name some specific things you want to talk to Jesus about. What things do you find hard to talk to Him about? What will make you more comfortable talking with Him?

   _____

   _____

   _____

3. Why do some people find it hard to pray? Why does a little talk with Jesus makes everything alright?

   _____

   _____

   _____

My Cu*t*e Daughter

_____

_____

_____

_____

_____

_____

_____

_____

_____

_____

Covered Until The End

It's Time...

Don't Live in the Past

"Then he waited yet another seven days, and sent out the dove; but she did not return to him again."
Genesis 8:12

"Brethren, I do not regard myself as having laid hold of it yet; but one thing I do: forgetting what lies behind and reaching forward to what lies ahead, I press on toward the goal for the prize of the upward call of God in Christ Jesus."
Philippians 3:13-14

My eyes opened up to the sound of a little bird chirping outside of my bedroom window. My initial thoughts surfaced around the idea that spring looms around the corner. But as I laid in bed for a few moments contemplating the thought, my mind wandered to the story of Noah and the ark. Why? Because the Lord works in mysterious ways.

So how does the chirping bird relate to Noah and the ark? Remember Noah built the ark to save himself, his family, and animals from the flood sent by God. When the flood subsided, Noah opened the window of the ark and sent a dove to see if the water had abated, but the dove returned. He waited another seven days and again sent the dove. The dove returned with a freshly picked olive leaf in its beak signifying land. Yet, Noah waited for another seven days and sent the dove out again. This time, the dove never returned. God spoke to Noah telling him to get out of the ark. In other words, it's time.

The ark separated the past from the future. Noah's ability to enter into his future, a new season, meant obeying God and stepping out of the ark. It meant leaving his past behind. Noah built an altar to the Lord, and the Lord smelled the soothing aroma (Genesis 8:20-21). God blessed Noah and his family and provided all of their needs.

See, the chirping bird signifies a new season, and the ark illustrates Christ's death and resurrection. His grace preserved us from the flood of divine judgement. So, since He paid the price for our sins, we no longer need to keep drowning in the flood or staying in the ark of our past. New land awaits us—it's time to get out of the ark.

It's time to put away the old and bring in the new. Time to remove the stale and infuse something fresh. Time to clean out the garbage in our lives and fill it with His truth. Time to spring forward and enjoy the "light" more. Time to reflect on the greatest tragedy that ever took place, which displayed the greatest act of love—the death, burial, and resurrection of our Lord and Savior, Jesus Christ. It's time.

It's time for you to leave your past behind—past mistakes, regrets, and failures. It's time to reach forward to what lies ahead: cultivating your relationship with Jesus. Choose to obey God, and step out of the ark. Allow your life to resemble a sweet soothing aroma to the Lord, and expect His blessings on you and the provisions of all your needs. It's time.

Discussion Points

1. What makes it hard to leave the past behind?

   _____

   _____

   _____

2. What does it mean to clean out the garbage in your life?

   _____

   _____

   _____

3. How can your life smell like a sweet soothing aroma to the Lord?

   _____

   _____

   _____

My Cu*t*e Daughter

_____

_____

_____

_____

_____

_____

_____

_____

_____

_____

_____

Covered Until The End

Laugh Often
Laughter

"A joyful heart makes a cheerful face,
But when the heart is sad, the spirit is broken."
Proverbs 15:13

"Then our mouth was filled with laughter
And our tongue with joyful shouting;
Then they said among the nations,
'The Lord has done great things for them.'"
Psalm 126:2

On this journey of life, you will encounter serious life situations. During trying times, you will find that laughter can serve you well. When disappointments and failures occur, they open new doors. Laughter gives you a different perspective on things and helps you lighten up when faced with challenging situations.

We all tend to take ourselves much too seriously. Getting a laugh out of everyday situations reveals a well-developed sense of humor. It enables us to laugh at ourselves over something funny we said or did or laugh with others.

In fact, scientists studied the effect of laughter on people. They discovered that laughter prevents tension and anxiety from escalating. People who laughed often experienced positive effects on every organ in their body.

Laughter and spirituality go well together. Proverbs 17:22 says, "A joyful heart is good medicine, but a broken spirit dries up the bones." Proverbs 15:13 says, "A joyful heart makes a cheerful face, but when the heart is sad, the spirit is broken."

A joyful heart brings healing to your soul. Laughing represents a precious gift and blessing from God. It acts like a pebble tossed across a river spreading its ripples across the waters. But a joyless life brings sadness.

Don't take things too seriously. Use appropriate humor to invite fun into your life. A joyful heart reveals a joyful countenance that you cannot hide. Your face will show what your heart and soul feel.

So laugh long and loud. Laugh until your face and cheekbones hurt. Laugh until you roll on the floor with your hands holding your stomach muscles. Laugh until you cry. Laugh often!

Discussion Points

1. Give an example of something you said or did that made you laugh at yourself.

   _____

   _____

   _____

2. What does the following statement mean: "Laughter acts like a pebble tossed across a river spreading its ripples across the waters"?

   _____

   _____

   _____

3. Give examples of appropriate humor versus inappropriate humor.

   _____

   _____

   _____

My Cu*te Daughter

_____

_____

_____

_____

_____

_____

_____

_____

_____

_____

Covered Until The End

Enjoy Life, Take Time to Play and Have Fun

Be Frivolous

"The thief comes only to steal and kill and destroy; I came that they might have life, and might have it abundantly."
John 10:10

*"Surely goodness and lovingkindness will follow me all the days of my life,
And I will dwell in the house of the LORD forever."*
Psalm 23:6

Compared to eternity, your earthly life only spans a few decades. We get a few years to live here on earth, so spending them unwisely results in a waste of time. When God says, "Your earthly time is up," it's done. So, take heed to the saying, "God's gift to us is life; the way we live that life is our gift to Him." View each day as a gift, and enjoy it.

Some think that living as a Christian diminishes the celebration of life. *You can't do this, or you can't do that.* But that mindset goes against what God's Word says. Jesus said He came to give you life and to give it more abundantly! He invites you to celebrate and enjoy the good life He gives.

As you pursue your goals and ambitions, work hard to excel. Go as far as you can in your endeavors, but always remember to play as you go. All work and no play make you dull and tiresome. Playing helps to refresh your mind, renew your strength, restore your vision, reclaim your youthfulness, and reset your goals.

Avoid doing dumb stuff. As long as playing remains sensible and wholesome, you can see God in a different light. It also provides God a chance to recreate the mundane routine of life and bless you with joy and freshness.

Take time to play and create fun. Act like a child again, and see the world through eyes of wonder. Skip and jump into the mud puddles after a rainy day. Bask in the feeling of soaked socks and muddy shoes. Sing while you work or complete chores. Be frivolous and make mundane tasks fun. Make silly spontaneous moments that make you squeal with excitement. Giggle, make up games, and invent stories.

Remember, you only get so many seconds, minutes, hours, days, months, and years to do what God created you to do. Free yourself and live. Pursue fun God's way, and enjoy the good life He gives to His children.

Delight in His creation and dance to His music so that when it's over, you can shout loudly, "What a wonderful and fun ride!"

Discussion Points

1. What does the following statement mean: "All work and no play make you dull and tiresome"?

   _____

   _____

   _____

2. Name some examples of "dumb stuff" you should avoid doing. How do you pursue fun God's way?

   _____

   _____

   _____

3. Name some frivolous (silly, not serious, or playful) things you do for fun.

   _____

   _____

   _____

My Cu*te Daughter

_____

_____

_____

_____

_____

_____

_____

_____

_____

_____

_____

_____

Covered Until The End

Oh, The Places You Will Go

Success and Prosperous Life

"This book of the law shall not depart from your mouth, but you shall meditate on it day and night, so that you may be careful to do according to all that is written in it; for then you will make your way prosperous, and then you will have success."
Joshua 1:8

The well-known Dr. Seuss book, *Oh, The Places You Will Go*, uses his signature humorous verses and pictures to address the ups and downs of life while encouraging one on the road to success.

"Congratulations! Today is your day. You're off to Great Places! You're off and away!
You have brains in your head. You have feet in your shoes. You can steer yourself
any direction you choose. You're on your own. And you know what you know. And
YOU are the guy who'll decide where to go. *Oh, the places you'll go!*"[ii]

He talks about seeing great sights and soaring to high heights; bang-ups and hang-ups; bumps and slumps; waiting and staying; being all alone; confronting enemies and strange things; yet you must continue on. The book concludes by saying, "And will you succeed? Yes! You will, indeed! (98 and ¾ percent guaranteed.)"[iii]

The book cover encourages parents to use it as the perfect send-off for children starting out in the maze of life regardless of their age or occupation. It inspires personal fulfillment for anyone and most find it a joy to read. But a greater book exists as the perfect send-off for a successful and prosperous life—the Bible. God uses His signature verses and pictures to truthfully address the ups and downs of life while encouraging you on the road to your destiny. Imagine the places you will go if only you read and obey the Book.

Joshua learned he needed to read the Book when God tasked him to lead the Israelites into the Promised Land. Joshua bore an awesome responsibility, so if anyone needed a formula for success, he did. I assume he received a lot of advice from many people, but his comfort and assurance came from the Lord speaking directly to him.

The Israelites experienced great sights and soared to high heights. They confronted bang-ups and hang-ups; bumps and slumps; waiting and staying; hard work and playing. Enemies and strange things came, yet they pressed on; but one thing God promised, never, NEVER being all alone. Unlike Dr. Seuss, God promised Joshua (and us) that He will not fail us nor forsake us (Joshua 1:5).

The Lord still speaks to you today through His Word. But in order for you to reach your destiny, you must do what the Book says. His Word tells you to live strong and courageously; carefully obeying what it commands you to do. "This book of the law shall not depart from your mouth, but you shall meditate on it day and night, so that you may be careful to do according to all that is written in it; for then you will make your way prosperous, and then you will have success" (Joshua 1:8).

So, read the Bible. Meditate on it. Memorize it. Understand its implications for the situations you face as you go to your destiny. Yes, trials lay ahead, but stay focused, and lean not on your own understanding.

And will you succeed? Yes! You will, indeed!
Not 98 and ¾ percent...But 100 percent guaranteed!

Discussion Points

1. What do you think the Lord is tasking you to do? Where is He leading you?

   _____

   _____

   _____

2. Name some places you want to go to or things you want to do. What obstacles might you face to soar to great heights to reach your destiny?

   _____

   _____

   _____

3. What must you do to stay focused? What did God promise you if you do?

   _____

   _____

   _____

My Cu†e Daughter

_____

_____

_____

_____

_____

_____

_____

_____

_____

_____

Covered Until The End

Live Courageously

Courage

"Be strong and let your heart take courage,
All you who hope in the Lord."
Psalm 31:24

"...greater is He who is in you than he who is in the world."
1 John 4:4b

Courage requires thinking and standing alone when following the crowd appears easier, safer, and right. But if you desire to do something important, meaningful, or significant with your life, you will need courage.

Standing up and standing tall demands inner strength that comes from how we perceive God, ourselves, and others. God will fight our battles, and He possesses all we need to win. We are His children, and the Bible tells us greater is He who is in us than he who is in the world.

Courage sits as a prime prerequisite for every accomplishment. Medals hung, records broken, plaques and pictures posted on walls and stands, rewards presented at events, are all due to courage. Faith grows deeper the more you step out and take a stand.

Courage requires inner fortitude to stand apart from the crowd. It takes strong character to remain consistent and diligent with your decisions. Standing courageously means risking ridicule or misunderstanding. Others may perceive you as a dreamer or a fool.

The story of David and Goliath represents a great example of courage. Even though David stood short and small in stature, faith and courage moved him to step out in front of the tall and large giant Goliath with only a stone and slingshot. To his own people, David looked like a fool and Goliath ridiculed him in front of both armies. Yet, David stood strong and defeated Goliath. His courage came from his faith and trust in God.

It took courage for Esther to go before the king without him summoning her in order to prevent the annihilation of her people. The penalty of this action could result in death. Yet, she learned that God chose her "for such a time as this." Her courage saved her people from death.

The lion in the Wizard of Oz desired the gift of courage. But he eventually realized he lived life as a victim of wrong thoughts. He thought that because he ran away from danger, he lacked courage. He confused courage with wisdom. Wisdom comes from the Bible—God's Word. The Bible gives you wisdom on what it means to live bravely and courageously.

The world lacks people with courage to persevere regardless of the odds stacked against them. Choose to live courageously. Don't miss out on opportunities to stand up and rise against the waves pushing you back. Stand strong, and let the Lord lead you. He will provide the strength you need to face what He puts before you.

Discussion Points

1. What important or significant thing do you want to do in your life? What will you need to do in order to achieve it?

   _____

   _____

   _____

2. What does it mean to live life as a victim of wrong thoughts? How do you overcome this?

   _____

   _____

   _____

3. What does the following Scripture mean: "Greater is He who is in you than he who is in the world"?

   _____

   _____

   _____

My Cu†e Daughter

_____

_____

_____

_____

_____

_____

_____

_____

_____

_____

_____

Covered Until The End

Bark or Bite

Fear

"The Lord is my light and my salvation; Whom shall I fear?
The Lord is the defense of my life; Whom shall I dread?"
Psalm 27:1

"In God, whose word I praise, In God I have put my trust;
I shall not be afraid. What can mere man do to me?"
Psalm 56:4

During their early years, my son Ryan and his wife Dani owned two dogs. Honey, a pure-bred pit bull, sported a strong, full-grown, muscle-toned body. Biggie packed a pint size body indicative of a chihuahua. Yet, you would never know it by his bark.

One day, I saw Ryan place a big bowl of food on the floor for the dogs to eat. Immediately a loud vicious barking from Biggie resounded as he blocked Honey from getting any food and prevented her from eating! This four-pound chihuahua hovered over the bowl eating and barking voraciously while Honey kept her distance and whimpered. I watched in amazement. This proved unbelievable since Honey towered over her as a big pit bull.

Did Honey know her identity? Did she understand the power and strength pit bulls possessed? If she did, she would realize that Biggie might cough up a big bark but produce very little bite. But until Honey recognized and accepted this reality, Biggie's barks evoked fear and prevented Honey from getting what rightfully belonged to her. Honey possessed everything she needed to get to the food, but chose not to use it.

Sadly, in a lot of ways, we mimic Honey's behavior. We allow Satan to bark at us as we keep our distance and whimper. He holds us hostage dictating our perspective and determining our actions. He keeps us in fear. Fear of our past mistakes and failures. Fear of chasing our dreams. Fear of meeting commitments. Fear of living alone. Fear of taking a stand for Godly principles. Fear of stepping out on faith. His bark sounds loud and ferocious, and it prevents us from receiving what rightfully belongs to us.

Do you know your identity? Do you understand the power and strength you possess through Christ? The spirit of fear comes not from Him. 2 Timothy 1:7 teaches us this truth saying, "For God has not given us a spirit of timidity, but of power and love and discipline." Jesus provides you with power through His Word to defeat Satan. Yet, sometimes like Honey, you may refuse to utilize it. However, when you decide to remove fear and stand on God's Word, you too will recognize that Satan barks big, but bites little. Let him whimper and flee instead of you.

The Bible uses the phrase "fear not" 365 times (conveniently one for each day of the year). God desires for you to know He will help you with all your fears. Replace them with the greatest fear and the first principle of wisdom—the fear of the Lord. Just ask Him to help you when your fears arise. If you feed your faith, you will starve your fears. With Jesus, you never need to be afraid.

Discussion Points

1. Name some things you fear that keep you from doing what God wants you to do?

_____

_____

_____

2. How do you overcome these fears?

_____

_____

_____

3. How do you feed your faith to starve your fears? What does that mean?

_____

_____

_____

My Cu†e Daughter

_____

_____

_____

_____

_____

_____

_____

_____

_____

_____

_____

Covered Until The End

Boldly Go Where No Woman Has Gone Before

Explore the Unknown

"Now the Lord said to Abram,
'Go from your country,
And from your relatives
And from your father's house,
To the land which I will show you…'"
Genesis 12:1

At the beginning of each new year, many people make New Year's resolutions. Some desire to get back into shape after eating tons of food from Thanksgiving through the Christmas season. Some resolve to read more, do more, spend more time with certain people, and the list goes on.

Our intentions to try to do something better usually fails or dwindles over time. Most of the time, we resolve to do something simply because someone else or the media tells us what we should or could do to make a change that they think proves best for us. They even do a great job convincing us that whatever we resolve to change, we really need it. The real question to ask is, "What does Jesus desire from me?"

Maybe He's asking you to do something new or scary which makes you hesitant, uncomfortable, or feeling ill-equipped to do. The Star Trek series used a statement at the end of their opening dialogue emphasizing this point. If you followed the series as a "Trekkie," you will be familiar with the line. It says, "to boldly go where no man has gone before."

Wow! Do we as Christians really boldly go where the Lord asks us to go? Forget the boldly part, do we even go?

You must decide to follow the Lord's calling and explore unknown territories that may prove uncomfortable. Seek the Lord's will at all times and for every area of your life, not just on New Year's Day. According to Genesis 12:1, He instructed Abram to leave his home and go to a foreign unknown land to fulfill a specific purpose. Abram acted on faith without knowing all the details. His obedience led to his blessing.

Ask Jesus what He wants from you. Whatever He desires, you can be confident that you will achieve it. It will occur by His power and not yours. Whatever He wants to get from you, He knows how to do it. Explore life with Him. Let Jesus guide you to new situations and new adventures. Stand willing to "to boldly go where no woman has ever gone before."

Discussion Points

1. Why do you think most New Year's resolutions fail?

_____

_____

_____

2. What new opportunity do you think the Lord is leading you to?

_____

_____

_____

3. What holds you back? What must you do to boldly go?

_____

_____

_____

My Cu*t*e Daughter

_____

_____

_____

_____

_____

_____

_____

_____

_____

_____

_____

_____

Covered Until The End

Count Your Blessings
Contentment

"Not that I speak from want, for I have learned to be content in whatever circumstances I am. I know how to get along with humble means, and I also know how to live in prosperity..."
Philippians 4:11-12a

"Make sure that your character is free from the love of money, being content with what you have; for He Himself has said, 'I will never desert you, nor will I ever forsake you'..."
Hebrews 13:5

God promised to provide for your needs, so if you possess food, clothes, and shelter, count your blessings. Take a pen and pencil and write down all He provides, and discover the outpouring of His goodness. You will see the vastness of His grace to you—giving you more than enough.

Rest content with God's provision. You must make money in this world to purchase goods and live. But the Bible says to free yourself from the love of money. Don't chase after it just to obtain more or to get rich. The love of it will cause you grief, not joy. You can experience joy whether you possess a little or a lot of money.

You must remember that a joyful and abundant life does not revolve around the accumulation of things. You will take nothing with you when your days end. A blessed life comes from gratitude. Gratitude leads to contentment. Knowing the source of your blessings keeps you grounded.

What if you earn a nice living and become wealthy? If you earned it legitimately, give thanks, and don't allow anyone to place guilt on your achievements. God gave it to you, so thank Him for it. Just avoid keeping it all to yourself. God blessed you with it, so give it back to Him by sharing with others. The more He blesses you to make, the more He expects you to give.

Avoid greed. Greed presents itself as an unhealthy desire for more. You crave, thirst, and strive for more, more, and more, never reaching the state of satisfaction. Normally the "more" results in something harmful to you. Jesus warns us to stay on guard for this, for it will lead to painful consequences.

Learn contentment. It's okay to work hard to make a good living. Just be aware of running after the success and prosperity of this world. Enjoy life, and let God fill you with His wonderful gifts. Thank the Lord for His provisions. He passes out the blessings and knows what each of us can handle. There's an old familiar hymn that states it best. It simply says:

> Count your blessings, name them one by one;
> Count your blessings, see what God hath done
> Count your blessings, name them one by one;
> Count your many blessings, see what God hath done.

If you spend more time counting your blessings, the paper and the ink in the pen will run out before you complete the count. As you name them one by one, you will experience contentment and gratitude for the Lord's bountiful provisions.

Discussion Points

1. What do you think would happen if you drank a glass of salt water? What if you drank several glasses? What painful consequence might you experience? How does this relate to money?

_____

_____

_____

2. How do you learn contentment?

_____

_____

_____

3. Think about your life. Name some of your many blessings.

_____

_____

_____

My Cu†e Daughter

_____

_____

_____

_____

_____

_____

_____

_____

_____

_____

Covered Until The End

Don't Give Up
Determination/Persistence

"Blessed is a man who perseveres under trial; for once he has been approved, he will receive the crown of life which the Lord has promised to those who love Him."
James 1:12

"Brethren, I do not regard myself as having laid hold of it yet; but one thing I do: forgetting what lies behind and reaching forward to what lies ahead, I press on toward the goal for the prize of the upward call of God in Christ Jesus."
Philippians 3:13-14

The old saying *persistence pays off* remains true. A valuable technique to successful living lies in sheer determination. You must decide to hang tough regardless of what happens. You must prepare yourself to pay the price when facing difficult situations that challenge you to the core.

Persistence and determination push you to stay the course. You will need these qualities in your educational studies, in working with people, in your career, in ministry work, and in making personal decisions that conflict with the world's standards. You will need to hang tough especially when everything looks bleak and you just want to give up. You may want to quit simply because someone says to quit or someone disagrees with you. Even during those times when you feel beat up or down-right tired, never fold up. Instead, hold up, trust God, and press on.

Visualize your goal, and just determine to get there. If you do, you will find or create a way to keep going. Take the first step and then the next. Step by step you will get to your goal. Stick to it, and God will honor your persistence and determination.

You only conquer the desire to give up by continuing on. When you feel like giving in to defeat, press on toward the goal. You can accomplish anything the Lord places before you if you stick to it. He will help you to reach your objectives.

Life entails a series of ups and downs, and not everything will turn out the way you think. You will experience disappointments and setbacks. But God provides comebacks so when you fall, get up and start again with more determination than ever. God loves you, and He will lift you up. If you persevere in your walk with Him, He promises a blessing awaits you for your faithfulness.

Discussion Points

1. Name some personal decisions that you will need to make that require determination and persistence.

   _____

   _____

   _____

2. Give an example of a time when you wanted to give up.

   _____

   _____

   _____

3. What happened when you trusted God, hung in there, and pressed on?

   _____

   _____

   _____

My Cu*te* Daughter

_____

_____

_____

_____

_____

_____

_____

_____

_____

_____

_____

Covered Until The End

93

God's Warning Signs
Temptations

"Let no one say when he is tempted, 'I am being tempted by God'; for God cannot be tempted by evil, and He Himself does not tempt anyone. But each one is tempted when he is carried away and enticed by his own lust. Then when lust has conceived, it gives birth to sin; and when sin is accomplished, it brings forth death."
James 1:13-15

"No temptation has overtaken you but such as is common to man; and God is faithful, who will not allow you to be tempted beyond what you are able, but with the temptation will provide the way of escape also, so that you will be able to endure it."
1 Corinthians 10:13

Power, pleasure, fame, and fortune seek to destroy us. These four forces appeal to our human appetites. We strive to control everything, do whatever it takes to make us happy, get a name for ourselves and get rich quick. These temptations dangle the deceitful carrot in front of us and when we bite, we plunge into deep despair.

God knows our fleshly weaknesses. The Scriptures and the Holy Spirit give us warning signs so that we can turn away from the bait before we sink. The Scriptures tell us how to live life wisely. The Holy Spirit instructs, guides, and reminds us of God's Word. He convicts us when we head in the wrong direction. He helps us distinguish between wise decisions versus foolish ones, good versus evil, and right versus wrong. He guides us to make the right choices.

Everyone lives with weaknesses. Openly admit them, and memorize Scripture to help you overcome them. Temptations will always exist; it's yielding to them that produces the sin. I found this comical poem that my father kept in his wallet to remind him of a temptation he faced—driving too fast. The unknown author of this poem, Sing While You Drive, simply reminds a person of the consequences of yielding to this temptation. It reads:

At 45 miles per hour, sing, "Highways Are Happy Ways"
At 55 miles, sing, "I'm But a Stranger Here, Heaven Is My Home"
At 65 miles, sing, "Nearer, My God, To Thee!"
At 75 miles, sing, "When the Roll Is Called Up Yonder, I'll Be There"
At 85 miles, sing, "Lord, I'm Coming Home"

So, avoid things, people, places or situations that cause you to yield to temptations. When they come, God remains faithful, and He always provides escape plans. You can walk or run away from temptations. Once you know what tempts you, guard your heart and cultivate a plan to deal with the specific temptation.

Rejoice when the Holy Spirit convicts you. Don't ignore God's warnings and push your convictions aside. His inner voice tries to prevent you from taking an inappropriate action or behavior that will only result in hurt and pain. Listen to what He says and take the correct action.

Discussion Points

1. What does "the deceitful carrot" mean?

   _____

   _____

   _____

2. Give an example of a temptation and yielding to it.

   _____

   _____

   _____

3. What temptation do you face? What plan can you cultivate to prevent yourself from yielding to it?

   _____

   _____

   _____

My Cu⸸e Daughter

_____

_____

_____

_____

_____

_____

_____

_____

_____

_____

Covered Until The End

Don't Worry About Tomorrow
Anxiety

"So do not worry about tomorrow; for tomorrow will take care for itself. Each day has enough trouble of its own."
Matthew 6:34

"Trust in the Lord with all your heart and do not lean on your own understanding. In all your ways acknowledge Him, and He will make your paths straight."
Proverbs 3:5-6

"When my anxious thoughts multiply within me,
Your consolations delight my soul."
Psalm 94:19

A familiar song says *Don't worry, be happy.* However, in today's environment, we find it difficult sometimes to remain happy and positive. We live in a very hostile world with negativity all around us. Headlines in the news fill us with all that goes wrong, the bad, and the ugly. We focus on the missing things in our lives and what we lack. It comes as no surprise that all this negativity affects us.

Strong feelings of anxiety stem from a negative mindset. If enough negative information seeps into you, anger, resentment, and fear surface which lead to a state of anxiety. Many things you worry about never happen, and when you worry excessively, small things become large, scary shadows of doom.

It's okay to be concerned. Concern recognizes the issue and seeks to find ways to control it. Worry controls you. If an issue or problem keeps you up at night, causes illness to your physical or mental well-being, or prevents you from functioning throughout the day, then it's worry.

Jesus commanded us not to worry. When we worry, we sin. We basically communicate to Him a lack of trust. Instead, He told us to trust Him with all our hearts and not to lean on our own understanding—our thoughts and feelings. Yes, feelings exist, but they should not dictate our responses. He wants us to acknowledge Him as Lord of our lives and trust Him intimately. If we use the Word and pray for His guidance, He will remove our anxiety and make things clearer as we move toward our destination.

Don't waste time worrying. Worrying only leads to non-productivity. Trust God with all of your life. Hang on to His Word, and expect the best. An old adage says, "Faith refuses to use today's time to worry about tomorrow."

Discussion Points

1. What do you worry about? Why?

   _____

   _____

   _____

2. Why should we not worry?

   _____

   _____

   _____

3. Psalm 94:19 says, "When my anxious thoughts multiply within me, your consolations delight my soul." What does that mean?

   _____

   _____

   _____

My Cu*te* Daughter

_____

_____

_____

_____

_____

_____

_____

_____

_____

_____

_____

Covered Until The End

Be Responsible
Accountability

"So then each one of us will give account of himself to God."
Romans 14:12

"And there is no creature hidden from His sight, but all things are open and laid bare to the eyes of Him with whom we have to do."
Hebrews 4:13

We live in a world faced with financial, family, and work stresses that exhaust the best of us. Sleepless nights and endless to-do lists add pressures to everyday life. But nothing goes hidden from God. He sees and hears it all, and He holds us accountable for careless words, remarks, and inappropriate actions.

Words spoken out of frustration, fear, or anxiety tend to come across as harsh and hurtful. When angry or upset, we let down our guard and spit out inappropriate remarks. We engage in thoughtless actions revealing less-than-Christlike behavior. Ugliness spills out for all to see.

So how do we keep it together? First, remember we all fall short of the glory of God. We need help because we cannot correct this problem on our own. Our help comes from Jesus Christ, our Savior who became accountable for our sins when He went to the cross. Now, He requires us to confess our sins, meaning we must tell Him what we did wrong, and He will forgive us.

Second, we need to include people in our lives who hold us accountable. These include a few trusted and loyal people we select to examine, correct, and counsel us. They ask the difficult questions and bring truth and wisdom to the situation.

If you desire to live responsibly and be accountable for your words and actions, you must confront your wrong behavior. Remain available, teachable, and open to wise counsel. Commit to hearing or admitting the truth no matter how painful or hurtful. Do the required action to correct or remedy the situation or inappropriate behavior.

In today's society, a lack of accountability prevails. But each person will give an account to God. Remember what Jesus did for you and how He continues to intercede on your behalf. Give those who earned the right to come alongside of you to walk with you to prevent you from making unwise and sometimes dangerous decisions.

Discussion Points

1. Give an example of a time when your behavior did not reflect Christ. What did you say or do? How did you feel?

   _____

   _____

   _____

2. Name a few trusted and loyal people in your life that hold you accountable. Give an example of how one of them helped you in a situation.

   _____

   _____

   _____

3. Name some things in your life that you need to take accountability for? Why?

   _____

   _____

   _____

My Cu†e Daughter

_____

_____

_____

_____

_____

_____

_____

_____

_____

_____

Covered Until The End

Manage Money Well
Stewardship

"I know every bird of the mountains,
And everything that moves in the field is Mine.
If I were hungry, I would not tell you,
For the world is Mine, and all it contains."
Psalm 50:11-12

"But you shall remember the Lord your God, for it is He who is giving you power to make wealth, that
He may confirm His covenant which He swore to your fathers, as it is this day."
Deuteronomy 8:18

Grasp this basic but profound fact: God is your ONLY source. He uses everything else as resources. Everything comes from Him. He owns everything! You own nothing!

You hold the role of a steward—a manager of all He generously gives you out of the goodness of His heart and that includes money. God wants you to prosper. In fact, He gives you the ability to make money. Use it wisely and glorify the Lord. Use it for good and the good of others. So how do you glorify God with your money? Three basic principles will help you practice stewardship His way.

#1 – Give. Honor God first with the tithe, the ten percent of your earnings. The tithe is holy to the Lord and belongs to Him. It reveals your trust in God. Most people miss the fact that it all belongs to Him anyway, yet He leaves you with the ninety percent to use as you please.

#2 – Save. Honor yourself for your work and effort you put in each day. When you work hard, you should reward yourself for a job well done. Save a portion of your earnings and use it at a later time for emergencies, rainy days, or future desires of your heart.

#3 – Spend. Use a portion of your money to meet your basic everyday needs such as food, clothing, and shelter. Once basic needs get met, you can spend some on your wants which are higher levels of your needs. For example, if you started out in an apartment, now you might buy a small house. After you get some of your wants, then you can advance to your desires. Instead of a 2-bedroom house, you can get a 4-bedroom house in a better community or take that dream vacation. Spend also to help others out when needed.

Whatever income the Lord gives you, little or much, remain faithful. Practice biblical stewardship. Thank God for the income, and maintain a right relationship with your money. Give to God first, save for yourself, and spend for your needs, wants, and desires. Help others out when you can. Always give willingly. God loves a cheerful giver.

Money talks. The way you manage your money speaks volumes about your values and priorities. One day, the Lord will require you to give an account. Jesus will review your stewardship of His money. He will assess how you used it for good and His glory.

Remember the source of all your money and possessions. View money for what it is: A resource to honor God; a method to fulfill life's obligations; and an opportunity to do good for others.

Discussion Points

1. If God owns everything, why does He desire the tithe?

   _____

   _____

   _____

2. Give an example of how you should manage your money if you received $100, $1,000, or $10,000? Calculate the tithe. What would you do with the other ninety percent?

   _____

   _____

   _____

3. Luke 16:10 says, "He who is faithful in a very little thing is faithful also in much; and he who is unrighteous in a very little thing is unrighteous also in much." What does this verse mean? How do you maintain a right relationship with your money?

   _____

   _____

   _____

My Cu_te Daughter

_____

_____

_____

_____

_____

_____

_____

_____

_____

_____

_____

Covered Until The End

See the Glass Half Full
Optimism-Positive Attitude

"So he answered, 'Do not fear, for those who are with us are more than those who are with them.' Then Elisha prayed and said, 'O Lord, I pray, open his eyes that he may see.' And the Lord opened the servant's eyes and he saw; and behold, the mountain was full of horses and chariots of fire all around Elisha."
2 Kings 6:16-17

How do you see this world? What type of outlook do you hold? When faced with challenges, do you see grasshoppers or do you see giants? It really depends on the focus of your vision. We all desire 20/20, perfect vision, which really means normal vision since you require no aids to see better. Eyeglasses or contact lens help bring a person's vision to 20/20.

What about your spiritual vision? Do you see or understand what an average individual sees or comprehends when you read Scripture? Do you desire to have perfect (mature) spiritual vision—the ability to see Him more clearly?

The Lord provides aids to use such as ministers, teachers, study guides, study groups, and study partners to help us see through spiritual eyes better. Our greatest resource lies with the Holy Spirit who illuminates God's Word to us. God provided this divine process whereby He causes the written revelation, His Word, to be understood by the human heart.

Sometimes we miss so much when God brings newness into our lives because we fail to open our eyes to a greater understanding of Him. Remember the story of Elisha when the king of Aram warred against Israel and sent a great army to circle the city. Elisha's servant cried out in despair as he looked upon the great army. Elisha prayed for his servant's eyes to be opened. If your focus centers around God's divine presence, almighty power, and His sovereign plan, you will see beyond what others and your naked eye reveal in spite of obstacles.

Your vision also affects your attitude. When you look through the lens of God, you will look on the bright side. You develop an optimistic positive attitude. This type of outlook allows you to see clearer, farther, and more focused. It delivers clarity of direction and removes negativity. You see the glass half full versus half empty. So, while others worry about the thorns and thistles of a rose bush, you see, touch, and smell the beautiful varied colored roses God created.

Optimistic people realize that hostility and negativity both exist in the world. They face harsh and challenging situations like everyone else. They just respond to them differently. They hang tough when the going gets rough and anticipate the best possible outcomes. Their determination to see things differently helps them strive to construct actions that deliver positive results.

In tough situations, they refuse to panic or throw in the towel. They say "yes" when everyone else says "no." They say "we can" when most say "we can't." They look through eyes of faith. Their optimism leads to achievement and making all things possible. They maintain perfect vision which requires ongoing trust in the presence, power, and plan of God.

Discussion Points

1. How do you see the world? Why?

    _____

    _____

    _____

2. What does it mean to see the glass half full versus half empty? Give an example.

    _____

    _____

    _____

3. How can you develop an optimistic positive attitude or help someone else despite what's happening in the world today?

    _____

    _____

    _____

My Cuᵗe Daughter

_____

_____

_____

_____

_____

_____

_____

_____

_____

Covered Until The End

Phenomenal Woman

Fulfilling Your Destiny

"For we are His workmanship, created in Christ Jesus for good works, which God prepared beforehand so that we would walk in them."
Ephesians 2:10

Phenomenal Woman is a well-known poem by Maya Angelou. The poem begins by saying, "Pretty women wonder where my secret lies. I'm not cute or built to suit a fashion model's size."[iv]

The second line in the first stanza may strike a nerve, "I'm not cute or built to suit a fashion model's size." But you must read the entire poem to capture the essence of Angelou's statement.

Maya may lack the label of cute based on the world's standards of beauty, but she definitely felt "fearfully and wonderfully made" in the Savior's eyes. Reading the entire poem convinces you that she knew she was a phenomenal woman—regardless of the world's view.

Ephesians 2:10 states, "For we are His workmanship, created in Christ Jesus for good works, which God prepared beforehand so that we would walk in them." Maya lived as God's masterpiece and instead of wasting time worrying about the world's perception of her, she focused on fulfilling the plan that Christ prepared for her. She refused to let the world's view stop her from walking in her destiny.

Angelou burgeoned as a prolific American author, poet, dancer, and singer. She published seven autobiographies, three books of essays, and several books of poetry. She received credit for a list of plays, movies, and television shows spanning more than fifty years. She acquired dozens of awards and over thirty honorary doctoral degrees.

She accomplished all of this without falling prey to the world's view of her outward appearance. She knew she fell short of the epitome of worldly beauty. For a while, she struggled with beauty and image. After all, she suffered from sexual abuse at a very young age. Believing her voice killed the man who raped her, she became a mute. Ironically, her voice ultimately became a weapon for teaching and encouragement.

Maya Angelou exemplified the meaning of a phenomenal woman. She professed Christ and believed that she could do anything and do it well because of God's love for her. She overcame all of life's obstacles and excelled. She fulfilled her destiny.

Discussion Points

1. What causes you to struggle with your beauty and image? What can you learn from Maya Angelou?

   _____

   _____

   _____

2. What makes you a phenomenal Cu†e woman?

   _____

   _____

   _____

3. How can you use your divine design to fulfill your destiny?

   _____

   _____

   _____

My Cu†e Daughter

_____

_____

_____

_____

_____

_____

_____

_____

_____

_____

_____

Covered Until The End

Do You Hear What I Hear?
Remembering God's Truth

"I will give thanks to You, for I am fearfully and wonderfully made;
Wonderful are Your works,
and my soul knows it very well."
Psalm 139:14

A song usually sung around the Christmas season asks "Do you hear what I hear?" Jesus told His disciples that He would suffer and go to Jerusalem (Luke 18:31-34). He told them He would face crucifixion. They listened, but did they really hear? After all, Jesus claimed to be the Messiah, the King, the Savior—not someone destined to go through the shame of a crucifixion. No Messiah goes through the impending suffering Jesus described. They heard only what they wanted to hear despite Jesus' effort to prepare them for His death. Jesus' words fell on deaf ears!

These fifty-two devotionals emphasized the way God feels about you. God's Word continues to tell you that you are His **Cu†e** daughter, "fearfully and wonderfully made." You are His masterpiece. You are His marvelous work of art. You are His princess. He loves you with an eternal love, and He will equip you for His work and His glory. Do you hear what I hear?

Ready for more good news? Now that you know that you are Cu†e, what does it mean to be Covered Until the End? It means exactly what it says. God manufactured you and you belong to Him. He holds the warranty of your life. So when things break down and when the trials of this world cause you to lose your shine and luster, the manufacturer stands ready and able to fix any problem. In Hebrews 13:5, He promises to never desert nor forsake you. Do you hear what I hear?

Some just don't want to hear. Yet, they quickly hear what the world, media, and everyone else tells them. They believe they can't possibly be the beautiful, worthy, and valuable masterpieces He created! This may be the reason so many women forsake Him and go through so much suffering. They listen to so many lies and God's Word falls on deaf ears!

So, the question remains, "Do you hear what I hear?" Do you hear God telling you how "fearfully and wonderfully made" you are, and He loves you so much just the way He created you? Do you get tired of listening to lies preventing you from living like His masterpiece? Do you desire to stop wasting your life going through meaningless suffering trying to measure up to what everybody else thinks? Do you want to hear the truth and live victoriously?

I hope that after studying these devotionals, your soul knows the truth and knows it very well. I pray you truly hear what I hear and you live like the masterpiece He created. If you do, then proclaim to Jesus and the world,

I Am **Cu†e**
Covered Until The End

*"I will give thanks to You, for I am **fearfully** and **wonderfully made**;*
Wonderful are Your works,
*and my soul knows it **very well**"*
Psalm 139:14 (emphasis added)

Discussion Points

1. Do you hear what Jesus is telling you? What do you hear and believe?

_____

_____

_____

2. Why do you think it is so hard for some not to hear and believe?

_____

_____

_____

3. What can you do to help others to "hear what you hear" and believe?

_____

_____

_____

My Cu*t*e Daughter

_____

_____

_____

_____

_____

_____

_____

_____

_____

_____

_____

Covered Until The End

My Cute Daughter

My Cute Daughter

My Cu*te* Daughter

My Cu†e Daughter

My Cu*t*e Daughter

My Cute Daughter

My Cute Daughter

My Cu*te* Daughter

My Cute Daughter

My Cu𝆑e Daughter

My Cute Daughter

Endnotes

i   Jonny Diaz, More Beautiful You (INO Records, 2009).

ii   Dr. Seuss, Oh, The Places You'll Go! (New York: Random House, 1990).

iii Ibid.

iv Maya Angelou, "Phenomenal Woman" from Still, I Rise, (New York: Random House, 1978), accessed August 14, 2018, https://www.poetryfoundation.org/poems/48985/phenomenal-woman.

About the Author

Pat Noble is a disciple of Jesus Christ and owner of NOBLE COLLECTIONS, a Christian-based company engaged in selling products and services that educate, encourage, inspire and present moral messages to youth and adults. Through God's inspiration, Cu†e (Covered Until The End) is a premier brand created by NOBLE COLLECTIONS. Cu†e provides encouragement to teenage girls and women to help them develop strong positive images and self-worth. The company's mission is to guide individuals to their identification and relationship in Christ, so they can experience the truth and live out their God given purpose.

As a former independent consultant working with various corporate organizations, Pat specialized in workforce development and training. She facilitated and provided class-room instruction and training with expertise in the areas of leadership, empowerment, coaching skills, negotiation techniques, presentation and communications skills, diversity and systems teller training. Pat assisted in course curriculum development and other training-related activities to support optimum learning experiences. She was a speaker for public and on-site seminars and summits. Some of her clients included Verizon Communications Inc., SAVI Learning Inc. (Shell Oil Netherlands), Skill Path Seminars, and Wachovia Banks.

Pat is an active member of Oak Cliff Bible Fellowship Church in Dallas, Texas under the leadership of Dr. Tony Evans. From 1999 to 2017, she served as the youth drama leader. From 2007 to 2013, she served as the drama director for the church-wide productions and the director of the adult drama ministry. During that time, in collaboration with her son Ryan, they wrote, produced and directed ten major productions reaching audiences of eight thousand or more per event. The impact of these productions led over 500 people to Jesus Christ. She currently serves in the Special Events ministry.

She is the author and co-author of numerous drama skits. She is also the author of the book "Are You Cu†e" and launched her first independent production, "Covered…" in 2018 at the W.E. Scott Theater in Fort Worth.

Pat received a bachelor's degree from the University of South Carolina and a Master of Business Administration from the University of South Florida. She is married to Tony and they reside in Southlake, Texas. They are the proud parents of three children: Shawn (who is with the Lord), Branden and Ryan (Danielle) and three beautiful grandchildren, Noah, Mathai, and Ryan Judge.

CPSIA information can be obtained
at www.ICGtesting.com
Printed in the USA
LVHW022040271122
734119LV00006B/293